THE ULTIMATE AUDITION BOOK FOR TEENS 2

111 One-Minute Monologues

By
L.E. McCullough

YOUNG ACTORS SERIES

A Smith and Kraus Book

DEDICATION

To my parents who continually ask, "Where did this kid come from?" Someday it will make sense to all of us.

Contents

FOREWORD

Show Miss Manners a grown-up who has happy memories of teenage years. . . and Miss Manners will show you a person who has either no heart or no memory.

— *Miss Manners' Guide to Rearing Perfect Children*

Almost everything is double like that for the adolescent; their lies are true and their truths are lies, and their hearts are broken by the world. They gyre and fall; they see through everything and are blind.

— **Ursula K. LeGuin, *Stone Telling***

Live as long as you may, the first twenty years are the longest half of your life.

— **Robert Southey, *The Doctor***

What, precisely, is "teenage"? According to the dictionary: **Teenage.** *Adj.* Of, being or relating to people in their teens.

Okay, that's both helpfully vague and vaguely helpful. Once upon a time, you became a teenager at fourteen, then thirteen, now some people say twelve, but possibly even as early as eleven or ten or nine, if you think of some of the social behavior and verbal sophistication formerly associated with older teens now being exhibited by younger children. And at the upper end, if you join the Army at eighteen and routinely operate weapons of mass destruction, does that make you more or less of a teenager than your twenty-year-old counterpart who's still living at home, hanging out on the basketball court, and slagging fries at Mickey D's?

Thus, these monologues are not age-specific. Because no teen is so "average" that his or her experience can be quantifiable in terms of what's happening to him or her at a particular time. So don't worry about it. If you're a twelve-year old actor, it might be a good idea to try a monologue from an older character just to stretch yourself. Older actors can sharpen their versatility by taking on younger roles. Experiment, 'cause you're a teenager and that's cool.

Over half of these monologues are suitable for both male or female exponents, and even some marked specifically "male" or "female" can be easily altered to fit your circumstance. Feel free to change a word or two here and there, if needed, and to adapt a monologue to your gender or home town or personal history or situation. The more *personal* the monologue is to you, the more *power* you can summon in your delivery.

Why? Because power and personality are two things that define a monologue. A good monologue (i.e., a monologue that captures and holds the attention of your listeners) is all about *character*, all about crystallizing for just a vital few moments the essence of a character and expressing that essence in a novel, exciting, memorable manner.

A good monologue is an *effective* monologue, effective in compelling your audience to listen to you and only you, to be caught up and confined totally in the Moment of You. And yet at the same time to be transported beyond you to other people, other places, other times. Maybe even transported somewhere deep inside themselves. . . a place they might seldom venture, or thought they'd forgotten, or wondered if they'd ever reach.

The key to unlocking the character in a monologue? *Language.* Each one of us on this planet uses language in a distinctive way that imprints our uniqueness as thinking, sentient beings. The language we choose to relate to the world — and to ourselves — reveals much about who we think we are and who we think we can be. When combined with appropriate gesture and intonation, words allow the character in a monologue to emerge and take shape before your very eyes.

These monologues cover a wide range of situations, emotions, and people. Read them through, find what feels good to you, what feels right for your experience or the character you want to inhabit and express. Some set-up directions have been provided to enhance your understanding of the situation and event sequence, and you'll likely do these in mime, unless you really do have a basketball or cell phone or soft drink bottle handy. But to develop better acting technique, you should strive to do the monologue without props. It's a skill that will come in handy when you're at an audition and handed a fresh side that says: "walking on a tight rope above Grand Canyon carrying a stuffed platinum mongoose."

Above all, have fun meeting 111 new people. Each one of these monologues *is* a person, and they're waiting to talk to you, eager to let you know what's on their minds. Listen, and you'll definitely learn a few things about their world — and yours.

L.E. McCullough
Humanities Theatre Group
Indiana University-Purdue University at Indianapolis
Indianapolis, Indiana

FEMALE
MONOLOGUES

MY SPECIAL TALENT

They say you find true happiness if you focus on nurturing your special talent. *(holds up exacto knife)* My special talent is biology. Dissection, to be precise. But for some strange reason people don't think dissection is. . . *fun*. I mean, when was the last time I got invited to a dissection party? "Hi, Lisa, we're all sleeping over at Kimberly's tomorrow and want you to bring your collection of lizard spleens." *(sighs)* People act like I'm, you know, weird, just for wanting to get to the heart of the matter. See what's really inside things. Explore the unknown universe of a still-beating salamander heart! But I understand. Science is a lonely calling. *(raises blade aloft)* And I hear it calling me now.

TERMINALLY SKOOCH

(wrings a scarf in her hands) Just took off the training wheels on Brittany and Chantelle, yo, bump that, girlfriend, these princess shorties got my props — I vote them both in as full Kweens of Kleen! Took this hoser down like puddin, mucho phat! We were on study hall patrol, and Brittany saw him by the bagelria, scratching his fleawhiz, what a pile! Then Chantelle showed him some beak, and he was, like, stiffie-city and followed her round back, licking his eyebrows all the way to the loading dock where Brittany barked him with a rodeo flip. She was *off* the hinges, tadow! Always thought Britty-boo was a fronter, but she carved this cakebag, no diggity, I'm still dusting down and I was like, ten feet away, I mean, ketchup monsoon blowing out his grill, then Chantelle laid in *her* butter, and this toad was, whoa, terminally skooch, hardly a squeal out of him the whole time. Right on, Sister Nightingale! One down, another twenty thousand to go! These bums are all over the city. Like bugs! My dad got a judge to close their shelter downtown, so they just moved out here to leech off us! Mercy buckets, pops! (unrolls bloody scarf) Foo, I gotta get some franklins from my mom and buy a new flag — this one's all hoopty! Yuck, squished troll juice!

TIGHT AND DOWN

I take care — *good* care — of my squad. Cheerleader captain isn't a fluff chore. And I'm not even talking the physical punishment you put your body through. I'm talking keeping your squad motivated, keeping their minds clear, keeping them tight and down with each other. I'm talking maintaining the mental power and purity that comes from knowing their bodies are *your* body, their dreams are *your* dreams, their tears are *your* tears. Because one day, you'll be tested. And you'll find out you don't cheer from your lungs. You cheer from your gut.

W.W.J.D.

(displays bracelet) This? My boyfriend got it for me at a youth rally. W.W.J.D. — "What Would Jesus Do?" Wearing the bracelet reminds you to ask that question whenever you come up against a difficult moral issue. You just think about the issue the way He would, and the answer comes through loud and clear.

Like a couple weeks ago, our Bible group had just let out. Jeannie and I were waiting in front of the laundromat for her stepmom to pick us up, and we saw this white Bronco go down the street, realllllll slow. Two guys around our age, maybe a little older, were in it, and one had a Mr. Microphone thing and would get next to somebody and yell at them with the microphone, or say something real nasty and personal and shout it out all over the street. Then they'd laugh and drive off. Well, they kept coming back around three or four times, just messing with people and stirring up a lot of anger and fear. Jeannie said, "Look at those dork-butts!" And I said, "Girl, hush your mouth!" and held up my bracelet and said, "Think, Jeannie — What Would Jesus Do?"

Then they came around again, and this time they about startled a little boy into falling off his bicycle right into the gutter. They stopped at the light, and I looked at my bracelet and thought real hard about what Jesus would do, praise His merciful goodness, and I walked over to the car. The passenger had his window down, and they were both giggling away and I could smell alcohol so strong it nearly made me heave. "Give me that microphone, please," I said, and he just stared at me and started to giggle. I grabbed the microphone out of his hands and threw it down on the pavement and smashed it to pieces with one stomp. "In the name of our Lord Jesus Christ who chastened the Pharisees in the Temple, I condemn this instrument of the devil. Go and sin no more." He got a real mean expression on his face and started to open the door. I rammed my Bible into his mouth — hard — and he screamed and fell back into his seat, and I called out, "Matthew 21, 12 to 17, read it for yourself!" just as the light changed and the car sped off, a big gloppy streak of red whooshing out onto the white side panel. We didn't see them around anymore that night.

(fingers bracelet) Well, I don't know if that's *exactly* what Jesus would've done. *(smiles serenely)* I'll just have to ask Him when I see Him up in Glory.

LEAVE THE PRAYING TO US

(stands quietly a moment, then blesses herself with the Catholic Sign of the Cross) My friends are totally blown out. They can't believe it, but, yeh, I want to be a nun. I know what you're thinking, but it's *not* an anti-sex thing. As far as sex, I'm, well, let's not go there right now, okay? But look at *your* life as a teenager. Every minute of the day you have to do this, be there, buy that, even your so-called leisure time is programmed to the nanosecond. Coming up is all the stress on college, and after that, you're a shrieking hamster on the career wheel for the next forty years, and why? Why all the stress? Why all the pressure? What do you think you're accomplishing?

This order of nuns, they do just one thing all day, all night. They pray. It's like a radio request line, people send them "special intentions" to pray for, and the nuns do it all day, all night. For a murdered son, for deeper faith for children, for a daughter's brain surgery, for peace in Ireland, for courage to stay sober, for protection of all life, for a successful adoption, one prayer after another from all over the world, all day, all night, they keep praying and that's *all* they have to do.

I'll deal with the celibacy thing when I need to. But right now, I can't think of a better way to spend the next few years than filling the universe with good energy to balance the bad. *(shrugs)* It's a tough job, but somebody's got to do it.

ONLY A STUPID SLASHER MOVIE

My boyfriend really likes those slasher movies. They scare me. He says all the violence is fake, and nobody really gets hurt, it's just like riding a roller coaster at Six Flags, you get a rush and a cheap thrill. But they scare me. It's, like, people terrorizing other people and hurting them cruelly for no reason or for some bizarre revenge everyone is helpless to stop except by killing the killer, usually in a way even more evil than what the killer does. My boyfriend says it's all made up, and sometimes they have a moral lesson or whatever, and he keeps telling me over and over there's no reason to be scared of a stupid slasher movie. I guess he's right, it's only a stupid slasher movie. Maybe what really scares me, is how much he likes them.

WHERE ARE MY FRIENDS NOW?

I didn't think it would come to this. Though my friends warned me. I just can't believe some girl is going to beat me up after school today because I'm dating her ex-boyfriend. I mean, we're not really dating, just he asked me out, and I said, "Okay," and we went to the burger place on South Main for, like an hour in broad daylight. I mean, nothing physical happened or anything, we just talked and had a burger, and then she bumps me in the hall third period and says, "Bitch, I'm seeing you later round back!"

My friends say she's only scaring me. My friends say maybe she won't be there, or maybe I can call a cop and get a ride home. But she'll be waiting tomorrow. Or the day after, however long it takes, that's the way people like her are, they don't have anything to lose. I don't think she even goes to school here anymore. She just looks for people to beat up, jesus—

Where are my friends now, dammit!

A BABY IS A JOB

I didn't think there would be so much screaming. Or that she'd need so many diaper changes. The same day my boyfriend broke up with me, I found out I was pregnant. Now I'm alone except for my baby. If I'm lucky, I get three hours of sleep at night, not all at once. I have no money cause I quit work to go back to school, and there's no welfare in this state anymore. When the baby was born, I called her father and said, "You have a daughter." He was like, "No I don't. *You* have a daughter." Know what's really weird? When I meet somebody and they find out I have a baby, they always say "That is so neat!" Uh-uh. A car is neat, an outfit is neat — a baby is a job.

ONE TEEN IN TEN

One teen in ten. That's me. The one teen in ten who's a —
(whispers) lesbian. *(shouts)* Lesbian Everybody hear that? The
biggest thing I have to deal with is remembering it's not such a
big deal. My sexual orientation is only one part of who I am. I
have hobbies and interests the same as you other nine teens,
you nine straight teens. I like music — and not "lesbian" music.
I like to paint pictures of horses — and not "lesbian" horses. I
like cooking and camping and singing hymns and watching
Dawson's Creek and I even like to shop for dresses and put on
makeup. I'm just like you, really. Except when I hear somebody
sing "Baby, I want your love to shine for me," I'm probably not
thinking of the same kind of "baby' as you. Is that a problem
for anybody? I'm only one teen in ten.

ASK THE FASHION GODDESS

(presses button on console) Welcome to "Ask The Fashion Goddess," immediate and perfect advice for the terminally fashion-challenged. Hi, Meredith, what's your question for The Fashion Goddess?

(another voice) "Do navy blue and black together break a major fashion rule?"

Meredith, I have good news, and I have bad news. Good news, there are no hard-and-fast rules in fashion anymore! If it looks good to you, wear it! Bad news, navy blue and black are mega-dorkish and thoroughly offensive to me, The Fashion Goddess. If I see you on the street, I will mock and revile you! Next caller!

(another voice) "This is Tawney Sue from down here in Boxcar Willie's Trailer Estates, and I got these wicked cheetah-print go-go boots, but I am kinda lost with what to match em with."

Listen to me, girlfriend, and listen good: The urban cowpie look went out with yesterday's chili pork rinds. Save the cheetah, free the go-gos and stop watching *Hee Haw* re-runs! (punches console) Britney, you're on the air with The Fashion Goddess!

(another voice) "Is, like, glitter, you know, still, like (giggles) — in?"

Britney, my sweet, you are a simple, simple person with a simple, simple question. And the simple-simple answer is: YES!!! Always and forever, glitter is IN! Disco, Roller Derby, Mardi Gras, Queen for a Day, glitter is the essence of our nation's fashion heritage! Glitter is as American as cheese ravioli. Didn't President Lincoln use glitter bombs to defeat the British at Pearl Harbor? I think she did. Glitter absolves even the most fashion-impaired of their gooberness, and, Britney, if you truly — in your simple-simple heart-of-hearts — want to please The Fashion Goddess beyond all reason, fill a salt shaker with glitter and sprinkle it merrily-merrily on every single outfit you own. Whoops! That's all the time we have for tonight. Remember, ladies, good fashion is eternal — bad fashion is on sale at K-Mart.

CYBER-ROMEO

I died this morning. In homeroom. Mortally wounded by the piercing-dagger stares of forty murderous eyes. Every one filled to the brim with. . . with laughter!

Last night I was bopping through the chat rooms, okay, when I got a random message from some guy saying, "Hey, babe, what's stickin?" Maybe it was the full moon; maybe it was the cute way he made the smiley sign so one eye was, like, winking; maybe it was that my screen name is Wild Marble 123 and his was Mild Warble 321, what are the odds of *that*? — but we instantly bonded! Hearts en fuego! I was a puddle! I told him *everything* about me! Deep desires, primitive passions, sizzling secrets — everything, of course, except our real names. That would ruin the romance!

Then this morning, I'm telling Misty how I've met the Hunk of My Dreams, when suddenly this mega-jerk in front of me — who I have despised the entire semester — says loud enough so the whole class can hear: "Check the wacko stuff this chick was rappin at me online last night! I got a printout. Who wants to see?"

Everybody turns around, of course. And when he says *my* screen name, and I realize *this* was my cyber-romeo *aaahhh!* and Misty wails out, "You can't dis my best friend!" and slowly, oh-so slowly-slowly, I sink beneath the crushing weight of forty murderous eyes laughing me into the linoleum. Love stinks!

USING IT, LOSING IT

Everybody says it's no big deal. Just go with the flow, feel good about yourself, use common sense and basic medical precaution, it doesn't mean you have to marry the guy. Or even go out on a second date. Or even keep a straight face when, you know, he asks if it was good for you, too. You don't have to answer to anybody, they say. It's *your* body, girl! Use it or lose it!

Funny. I don't think of *not* having sex as losing something. Or keeping something, either — hanging onto that mysterious *it*, using *it*, losing *it*, doing *it*, getting *it* on, like *it* is what *I* am all about and nothing more. Nuh-uh. I may only be a teenager, but I think I've already figured out I don't want to have my life controlled by a pronoun.

SO OUTA HERE

When I started dating Rick, he was such a sweet guy. He always walked me to class and sent me little notes. He made me feel our friendship was really special. But lately, I don't know. Like yesterday, he was standing at the drinking fountain with some of his guy friends. I walked up and said "Hi!," and he glanced at me, then looked away, like I was a stranger. I asked him where he'd been at lunch, cause he didn't sit with me like usual, and he says in a real nasty voice, "I was shootin hoops with my buds. That all right with you, or do I gotta ask permission first?" His friends all snickered, and I just kinda slunk away. Then after school, Rick wants to hold my hand and walk me home like nothing had happened. Maybe it's just a guy thing, but it reminded me of how my dad treated my mom, and I'm thinking, nuh-uh, I am outa here. I am *so* outa here.

SO MELODRAMATIC

"Hi, Mom! Gorgeous day outside! That's a lovely outfit! You know, if you have to stay late at work tonight, I can make dinner. And pick up the dry cleaning, sure, no problem, oh, by the way, I'm sexually active, will you drive me to the clinic to get some birth control pills?"

Nope. Too blunt. She'll stroke out. And then I get a lecture. *(sighs)* How am I going to break the news? "Mom, I have but three weeks to live. Is it okay if Jeff and I, you know, hook up?"

Uh-uh, no way. *(stands at attention)* "Mother, there comes a time in every teen's life when she must seize her destiny, fulfill her ambition, bow to the will of the masses. The people have spoken, the nation is at stake — must begin having sex immediately."

Aaaauuggghh! This s crazy! wish could just be open and honest, but she'll *never* understand, *never* be rational, *never* — *(notices something down and to her right)* — what's this pamphlet on the dresser? *(picks up pamphlet, opens it)* "When Your Teen Is Having Sex." *(shouts offstage)* Mommmmm! You are *so* melodramatic!

ONE UP

I've been going out with my boyfriend for about five months now. And I thought we were kinda close. I mean, we talk about a lot of deep stuff, and we always have fun and lots of laughs. But about a month ago, I found out he cheated on me with some girl he met when he visited his cousin out of state. He said he was sorry, it just, you know, *happened*. So, two weeks ago, I bumped a guy I worked with last summer at Dairy Queen. It just, you know, *happened*. My boyfriend says I deliberately took revenge, but I didn't. I just thought, well, now we're even, no big dealio. So then, this week, he tells me he hit the kitten with this girl in his chem class, and, to me, that is straight-out revenge! It didn't just, you know, *happen*. He planned it so he could be one up and show me who's boss! I just don't understand guys at all. Everything's a competition with them. *(frowns, then smiles)* Except for you. I think you're different. *(reaches her hand out to cover another hand)* If you're not doing anything later, could you help me study my, um, anatomy homework?

THE NATURAL WAY

(holding a vitamin bottle, reads from label) "BUSTING LOOSE —
an all-natural, non-surgical, herb-based breast enhancement
vitamin." My boyfriend gave this to me for Valentine's Day. He
said it would mean more than candy or flowers. Very thoughtful, isn't he? *(reads from label)* "Revolutionary European formula *may* result in breast size increase of a full cup or more
when taken daily for several months." I guess he's thinking
we're in for a long-term relationship. *(reads from label)* "Let
21st-century vitamin technology help you achieve the bustline
you desire, the natural way." Hmmm. I wonder is there a vitamin to help achieve the boyfriend desire? Probably not. *(drops
bottle into waste can)* I don't think they could ever develop a
formula to increase brain size.

THESE TIMES

You know one of my favorite things to do? Go with my mom to the mall. No, we don't shop. We just sit and people-watch. We pretend we're on a jungle safari, like on those nature shows? And we're watching all these different species of human animals in their habitat — how they eat, how they walk, their mating rituals and greeting patterns, all the really bizarre and funny things people do at a mall, it's a trip! We make each other laugh so hard, we end up in tears sometimes and getting really strange looks from the security guards. I love my mom. I know that sounds weird for a teenager to say, but some day, when things get rough or I'm all alone, I'll be able to think back on these times and remember what it was like to laugh.

IN YOUR FACE

There's this guy in my history class who, like about once a day, gets up in my face, grins like a fool, and mumbles my name, then walks away, giggling. That's it. Is he just a basic wacko, or is this some special form of "guy language mating code" that means he likes me? Am I supposed to be impressed? How do I respond? Giggle back? Kick him in the shin? I have no idea! It's like, once I entered middle school, all the rules changed. I'm a contestant in this bizarro game show where the other players are playing a different game but you're the one who gets the pie in your face. Hey, maybe that's what I'll do. Next time he gets in my face, I'll smush a twinkie on his nose and see what happens. *(giggles)* Then *he'll* have to figure out what I meant by *that!*

RANSOM

I had just shut down the fryers for the night and closed the drive-thru window, when some dude with a ski mask walks in, gun shaking in his hand. Doesn't say a word but sticks the gun right in the new counter girl's face, her first day on the job, the barrel touching her forehead. "Put your gun down and walk away before you commit a grievous sin," she says. "You can walk in the light of the Lord and be free." He laughs and cusses her, then pushes the gun harder against her forehead. She tells him again, "Put your gun down and walk in the light of the Lord." There wasn't a flicker of fear in her face. He was shaking like a dang leaf, but she was calm as could be. "I'll pray for you," she says, her eyes shining with a beauty and a love for what she was saying to him. "I'll pray the Lord's mercy—" BAM! He pulled the trigger and shot her three times BAM! BAM! right through the head and a huge smack of light exploded before me, blinding me as he turned the gun on me. *(cringes, lowers head, shields eyes, and holds an arm across stomach)* I wasn't as brave as her. I couldn't look him in the eye, so I just got ready for a big blast of pain and thought of my parents and the unborn baby inside me and then heard the chamber click and the trigger snap — but nothing happened. He threw down the gun and ran out the store. *(straightens up)* The police checked the gun and said it was a misfire, nothing really wrong with it far as they could tell, just hadn't worked when he shot at me.

But it sure had worked on the new girl, who'd died thinking she could change this guy, change him right at this ultimate crossroad and lead him down another path. Now that was faith. That was *love*. And I was so stunned by that faith and that love, even more than seeing her die, that I quit drinking.

Quit doping. Quit being a dumbass and went back to school and got my diploma the same day my son was born. I took up a whole new way of life. And I took up her name. I called my little boy Ransom. That was all what was on her name tag — Ransom. I never knew her first name. But as long as he's in my life, she'll be there, too. Maybe some of her faith will stick with my boy, sometime when he really needs it.

THREE LITTLE WORDS

(curtsies, strikes a beauty pageant runway pose) Esteemed judges, worthy sponsors: It is an honor and a privilege to be a semi-finalist for Miss Teen Reconstructive Surgery Outlet Mall of Newberry! Three words that best describe me? Hmmm. . . let's see now, hmmm. . . that would be, well, hmmm. . . thoughtful! *(giggles)* That's one! Word number two that best describes me. . . ooooohhhh, I think it, nooooooo, more like, mmmmmm, I'd have to say, welllllll. . . impulsive! *(giggles)* And the third word that best describes me? Oooh, maybe, no, yes, it's on the tip of my tongue, possibly but not so much that but more like, mmmmmm, gosh-golly-gee, ohhhhhh-ummmmm-rrrrrrrr-ar-ar-ar-ar-articulate! *(giggles, curtsies)*

BREAK-UP CLUES

Relationships can be very mystifying for a teenager. You need to be attuned to every nuance, every subtle hint in the changing fortunes of your romance. For instance, how can you tell when your boyfriend is thinking about breaking up with you? Here's a top ten list of clues:

Clue Number Ten, he signals that your conversation is over by clamping his hands over his ears.

Clue Number Nine, when you're out walking, he begins singing and skipping merrily — several feet ahead of you.

Clue Number Eight, he starts calling you by your best friend's name.

Clue Number Seven, he asks you what gender you *really* are.

Clue Number Six, when you go to a restaurant, he refuses to be seated until he's eaten all the candy mints at the cash register.

Clue Number Five, when you're in the middle of a sentence, he pulls out a TV channel changer, points it at you and says "Mute!"

Clue Number Four, he says he'd like to have a heart-to-heart talk at a scenic location — the local landfill.

Clue Number Three, he forgets it's your birthday but asks if you can lend him a few bucks to buy a pizza for the guys watching the game back at the house.

Clue Number Two, he starts the conversation with "I have a slight confession to make. . ."

And the Number One Clue your boyfriend is thinking about breaking up with you — you've just finished paying for dinner, and he leaves the going-steady ring you gave him as a tip. And says loudly so the waitress can hear, "Oh, look, this check number is the exact same number as my cell phone!"

Happy romance, kids!

MALE
MONOLOGUES

TREASURE MAP

Coach said to me, "Dawson, you could be the best in the county, but you live too far deep inside yourself. Sometimes I look at you flailing away out there, I don't know whether it's *you* I see, or a *shadow* of you coming up to the surface for a quick breath before diving back under. I gotta have the whole man, good or bad don't matter, long as I know there's no part buried down where I can't find it when the game is on the line." I said, "Coach, if I come across a treasure map with an X-marks-the-spot, I'll let you know."

READINGS IN AMERICAN HISTORY

Me and Bucky went down to Methodist to see Ma yesterday. She's been on suicide watch and some detox, too, since Tuesday. At the bus stop, we seer a Asiatic girl, college student most likely, reading one of her school books and sitting there real small and slim and flowery-like, with long straight black hair shimmering like liquid black marble and floating a little wavy bit in the cool morning breeze. Then a big fat kid come up, just about Bucky's age, not even — torn blue jeans, black spike boots, dirty white T-shirt with ARYAN AVENGERS painted on it. Didn't even look at me or my brother but just spit on the ground right next to the girl's feet and yelled:

"Know what you are? Goddam slant eyes so goddam smart IQ can't even talk goddam English!"

Girl closed her *Readings in American History* book, a fine wisp of soft marble hair dangling across pink parted lips, and looked up at him real slow, studying him a second or two like he was a strange kinda bug just lit on her lunch:

"My eyes see you, sir, very well. You, sir, are A Racism."

Then she went back to reading her book, and the kid cussed some more and spit again and finally tromped off down the street trying to kick an empty beer can but missing by a good half a foot.

Bus come about a minute later, and all the way downtown I could tell Bucky was upset and not likely just by ma. I told him, I says, "Chill, bro, and don't get tweaked. You got plenty of time yet before you supposed to hate people for no damn reason at all."

FATHER'S DAY

He starts yelling, "If I had my legs, I'd knock that filthy tongue out of your head!" That's my dad, always some bogus excuse for not coming through. Even when he *could* walk, he was a drunken loser. Hell, I bet he *can* walk. I bet he's faking it, so he can weasel out of his child support and the lawyer stole his disability and mom's relatives won't support us. Hell, dad, that's *your* job! If you were a *decent* father, if you gave a *damn* about your son — you'd get your sorry ass up out of that wheelchair and knock me from here to next Tuesday!

BRAND NEW GAME

When it snowed yesterday I went down to the river, where we used to take our sleds when we were kids and pretend they were race cars and then tumble down the bank like fuel-injected, dual-quad Abominable Snowmen at the Indy 500, neck-and-neck in the final lap roaring out of the fourth turn straining for that checkered flag and a beauty queen's kiss — imitation immortality that would last til we got back to grandma's for grilled cheese and cocoa.

Yesterday, while I watched the snow quiet down the afternoon city noise, like the cool white washcloth your mom would lay across your forehead when you were burning up with fever, I saw a pack of little boys on sleds skidding down the bank and yelling and throwing snowballs at each other the way little boys do. The biggest one jumped up and hollered so loud he almost fell over: "Drive-by shooting! Drive-by shooting! I love this game! Smoke 'em! Smoke 'em! Smoke 'em!"

Suddenly, I needed a grilled cheese and cocoa really bad.

HUMAN ENGINEERING, INC.

So, yeh, last weekend my parents sent me to take some "apti-tude tests" at a place downtown called Human Engineering, Incorporated. For real! They're worried about my future. Must've found out I put down "Intergalactic Death-Metal Sex-Lord" on the career day preference sheet. But these Human Engineering dudes are cool. They say a word, and you shoot back whatever pops into your mind, like they say "database design" and you say "booger." *(chuckles)* They say "investment sales" and you say "oral prophylactic." *(snorts)* It was to laugh! Then you boink around awhile with puzzles, which reveal deep-deep personality secrets, like, if you can tie your shoes without looking — hah! been acing that since middle school! Finally, they show you pictures you write a sentence about. At first, it was like, gag-city — puppy dogs and sunsets and cheering sta-dium crowds and starving Third World children supposed to evoke emotional regurgitations from your empathy center. But then, all of a sudden, I just lost it. I mean, I was speechless. I looked at this *thing* up there on the screen for a long, *long* time. It was beautiful, it was hideous. I was thrilled, I was terri-fied. I couldn't believe my eyes. I couldn't look away. . .

It was a picture of me. When I was a baby. And had just started my whole life not knowing anything — but grabbing for it all. No fears, no worries, no hangups, just this grinning, shouting ten pounds of instant human saying, "Hey, world, here I come! Stand aside, cause I'm ready to ride!"

Human Engineering, yeh. Well, somewhere between the cradle and the skateboard, I got some circuits crossed. I see that now. I'm looking up ahead at the next chunk of my life, and I say this: It's time to go back to the drawing board.

WHAT PASSES FOR RESPECT

Me and Deric was buds for awhile. We'd go down by the rail tracks and look for snakes, break bottles, b.s. about cars and stuff. We was both dinky little guys, and Deric always talked about when he was grown up, he'd get respect from all the jocks who laughed at us now.

Awhile later, his dad died, and Deric got kicked outa school for hitting a teacher and setting fire to the tire shop on Warman. I never saw him no more till the end of last summer. He was standing on the corner each night down by the vacant lot next to the rib joint selling crack to whoever had the cash. Sometimes he'd flash a pistol or a knife and smile real big like he was in some badass gangsta movie.

Last Sunday morning Deric got shot in the head four times coming out of his mother's house by some bigger kids from the Belmont Street Posse wanting his business for themselves. I wasn't at the showing but my sister's boyfriend Herschell was, and he said the kid that ordered the hit bought Deric a brand new suit to be buried in. Even sent his mother a whole porch-full of flowers, just to show there wasn't no hard feelings.

Way things are round here in Stringtown these days, I guess you'd say that's what passes for respect.

KEEP IT REAL

Hell yes, I knew I was gonna get bagged up! What fool walks into a damn video store wearin a bright red doo-rag and hoody, stick a jumbo DVD in his tommies, stare the rent-a-pig in the face and think he ain't gonna get bagged up when he hit the beep-gate? That the whole show, homey! My uncle was standin right there, makin sure I stayed down with it, know what I'm sayin, he have my back all the way. Now the 18th Street organization, you gotta bang somebody to join them, but my peeps in the 2-1, all you gotta do to graduate from Baby G to OG is take a bust and do the time on your crime. Simple as that, jat, and you can tell the judge to pack his fudge while I keep it real here in the steel. Hey — who said you could be my damn lawyer, anyway?

THE RESPONSIBLE PARTY

No, your honor, I plead not guilty to all charges. Look, my old man said if I skipped school once more, he'd tear me a new one, you know what I mean? So me and Craig, we was on our way to school yesterday and we seen this girlie magazine on the side of the road, and Craig says, "Hey, my book report's due today in English!" So we spent awhile lookin through the magazine for some literature Craig could use, and by the time we found it and got to school, the doors was locked, and I says to Craig, "There's no way I can be absent again," so we figured we'd better get outa town and went down to Washington Street and stole a car, a real nice Honda. Got far as Rockville and run outa gas, so we held up a 7-11 and that took us to Vandalia, but then the state trooper chasin us was some crazy mother and forced us off the road into that old lady's front porch, I think she's supposed to live. Nosir, none of this woulda happened if I hadn't been late for school. It's my old man's fault. Throw his sorry drunk ass in jail! He's the responsible party!

A BABY IS A JOB

Yesterday, my girlfriend told me she was pregnant. I'm, like, slammin! Woo-hoo! Sure, I want to be a father — someday. I mean, hey, kids are neat! I'm one, aren't I? *(chuckles)* Except I think having kids is something girls get into easier. I'm not slick with all the cuddle-poo stuff, the naturing-nurturing, whatever they call it. I want a kid that's more like a dog, something you can roll around with, toss a ball to and they toss it back, *rrrrr!* *(growls, chuckles)*. Look, I'm sorry we goofed up with the birth control thing, nothing's a hundred percent, right? I know I'm responsible, but right now a baby is a job, and I don't think I'm, like, qualified to handle it. I'll pass on this one.

NEVER BEEN HAPPIER

No sir, never did make it to Eagle Scout, but I always liked the way I looked in a uniform. After mama and Terrell died I had to work. Did the busboy shuffle at the 16th Street Waffle House for sub-minimum wage. The night cook, Martha Ray Jean, would make us all the tastiest batch of strawberry grits flavored with a dash of Thunderbird. But clearin up after people and pretendin you gave a whup about which way the fork faced a napkin got kinda old after awhile. I knew there had to be more goin on in the world than that. One day I seen a bumper sticker said, "Join the Army, travel to exotic lands, meet interesting people — and kill them." So I did. And I never been happier in my whole life, bubba.

PUBERTY ALARM

(sleeping, snoring; jerks wide awake) Rrrrrinngg! Oh-no, my puberty alarm went off! For the twelfth time this hour! *Aaauugghhh!* It happened so fast. One minute I'm just a kid. Next minute, puberty strikes with a sledgehammer! *Ooo-mmpph!* The simple act of, say, eating an ice cream cone — nudge-nudge, wink-wink — becomes tinged with undercurrents, overtones, ennnn-tennn-dresss! One minute I'm just a kid, watching TV and digging on Xena Warrior Princess swinging that battle ax — *rrrrrinngg!* — puberty alarm, and *no* way am I watching Xena with my parents in the room! Uh-uh! Change channel to Barney, but it doesn't zap Xena from my pubosity-filled mind! Innocence abandoned, out the window! The alarm has rung, and I am soooooo wide awake every time I hear a girl speak, see a girl pass by, think of the word G-I-R-L, *yowwwwwwwwww! (exhales)* Sometimes, I just wish I could hit the snooze button on that alarm and go back to being a kid for awhile.

ASK THE FASHION DUDE

(presses button on console) Welcome to "Ask The Fashion Dude," immediate and most excellent advice for the terminally fashion-whipped. Say-hey, Douglas, what's your ka-westion for The Fashion Dude?

(another voice) "I'm going out with this girl for the first time, to dinner and a movie. What should I wear?"

Well, Doug-man, you failed to elucidate as to whether this girl is a bonafide hottie or a stone crusty. But that doesn't matter! The Fashion Dude is gonna play it close-up tonight and suggest you be on the safe side and wear something outrageous that deflects visual attention from her, cause if she's really a babe, you don't wanna spend the whole night with everybody staring at her. And if she's a crusty, you wanna be invisible, dude! Peace out! (presses button) Froggy, my man! Hit me with your best shot!

(another voice) "Say, Fashion Dude, have you ever designed your own threads?"

The Fashion Dude is a mondo style-setter. Just last week I found an old pair of paisley surf shorts in a locker at the bus station. Score! Took em home, turned em inside-out, okay? Now the normal zeke would stop there. But nottttttttt The Fashion Dude, who pushes the style envelope to the Utter Limits! Ready for some real amperage? I turned em upside down! Score! And I wear em as an over-shirt! Double Score! Pants above the waist! Fashion Dude has struck again, and noooooooo one is safe! (presses button) Next ques-ti-on-é!

(another voice) "This is Herb from South Side. They're having a dance at school, and the theme is Natural Wonders. What should I wear?"

Yo, Herb. First things first. If you're at a school with a lameoid dance theme like that, you need to transfer to a new school real fast. Or, worst-case scenario, maybe even graduate. "Natural Wonders"? Try dressing like a tree and stuffing alfalfa in your hi-tops. Not! To survive this extreme fashion emergency, I recommend — no, *command!* — a maximum dosage of fringe. Fringe absolves even the most fashion-gagged of their cheesitude. It's classy in a '70s-retro way; think David Cassidy meets Clint Eastwood at a Kiss concert. And super-handy if your belt breaks or you need to find your way back to — whoa-oh! Time's up for tonight, so happy trails to all you righteous snails, and remember: Good fashion is forever, and bad fashion is what your parents buy you for your birthday.

VOID WHERE PROHIBITED

As to my current State of Virginity — look, it's not about who I'm hooking up with, it's the thought that counts. And your thoughts on my behalf are deeply appreciated! But if you really *must* know the ugly non-details, check my web site: www-dot-I'm Ready for Action, Jackson-orgggggggggg! A veritable plethora of information revealing my hilarious romantic misadventures with the opposing gender, plus a special one-time contest offer from site sponsors for valuable cash prizes, if you can name where, when, and in what millennium I will surrender my virginity! Contestants must be under the age of reason and possess no social life of their own whatsoever to participate. Void where prohibited by good taste and something, *anything*, better to do!

A SHELL IS A WONDERFUL THING

(typing on computer keyboard, stops, stares at screen) I don't believe this! "My seventh-grade son is very shy and lonely. I'm afraid he's beginning to not like who he is. How can I help him come out of his shell?" *(looks up)* This is my mother posting to an on-line family shrink! Next she'll be putting up my naked baby pictures for auction at E-Bay! Well, excuse me, mom, but being in a shell isn't such a terrible thing. A shell can be very private. A shell can be very nurturing and protective. A shell can be a great way to look out on the world without having the world staring in at you watching your every move when you don't always know where you're going. What you call "shy and lonely," I call "keeping a safe distance between me and the insanity of the world" — *your* world. Okay, so I'm in a shell. It's not a prison. It's a refuge, a sanctuary. And I can walk out of it any time I want. Which I plan to when I feel the time is right. Like maybe when I'm about thirty.

AFFIRMATIONS

I am a happy, healthy, wholesome, beautiful, positive person. I am a unique and priceless person, coming from a unique and perfect pattern within me. I am an extremely well-liked and pleasing person. I am extremely successful in everything I do and say. I have complete and unconditional worth as a person in this universe. I give myself all the permission I need to do what I know is best. I trust and rely upon my excellent sense of judgement in everything I do. I am the best judge of what is best for me. I am fully competent and capable in everything that I decide to do. *(inhales, exhales deeply, then dials phone)* Hi, Jennifer, this is Bed Tartley, uh, Ted Bartley. Would you like to pro to the gom with me? No, gom to the pro, pro-prom-go-prom-you-me-Bed-no-Ted-will you go to bed with me — oh, hi, Mrs. Wilinski. Did Jennifer say when she'd be home? Thank you. *(hangs up phone, inhales, exhales deeply)* I am a happy, healthy, wholesome, beautiful — *moron!*

WHOSE BREATH

(holds basketball) This is a basketball. It's a simple thing. Piece of leather filled with air, makes it round and hard. *(bounces basketball)* A basketball is subject to the laws of gravity. Goes where it's thrown or punched or kicked or blown by the wind. Doesn't appear to have a will of its own, does it? But this basketball, this very one, was in the hands of my best friend Marcus when his heart gave out. When he fell to the court and hit his head and lay there, looking up at me, not breathing, probably not even seeing me pounding on his chest and shouting his name and screaming at him not to die. This basketball, this very one, was still in his hands, even as his face turned blue and his brain shut off and his soul left his body. He wouldn't let go of this piece of leather, he would not let go. *(raises basketball aloft)* And I look at it every now and then, and I keep thinking, the air that makes this thing be alive — whose breath did it take? Whose lungs did it steal *its* life from?

A REPUTATION TO PROTECT

Inside the barn it was dark except for a pair of flood lights shining down on the ring. The mayor's brother announced the next fight, and I looked into the ring, and Reedy the TV repairman Dad used to rent the storehouse to was dragging a dog out of a cage to face a pit bull one of the Kentucky guys had brought. Reedy's dog had a black-and-white face and funny brown splotch on his nose. It was Boo — our family dog we all thought had run away a couple months back.

I screamed at Reedy to let him go, but he just kept dragging Boo to the ring. I kept screaming, and everybody was yelling at me to get the hell outa the way, and I yelled for Dad and saw him trying to push his way toward us, but Reedy kept dragging Boo to the ring. I kicked Reedy in the leg, and he cursed at me and shoved me down, and then Dad was there, standing over me. "Hold on!" he shouted, and everybody shut up and stopped moving cause that's what you did when Dad shouted at you.

Dad looked at Reedy and poked a finger in his chest and said in a loud strong voice, "Don't ever lay a hand on my son again," and Reedy shrank back, and Dad reached down his hand to me, and I took it. He hauled me up on my feet and walked me outside. I was shaking, but he had his big hands firm on my shoulders, and I wasn't scared really, and everybody was still quiet except for all the dogs barking, and when we got outside I looked up at Dad, and he smiled.

And then he punched me in the gut so hard I fell on my ass and couldn't breathe without crying for an hour. "Go sit in the car," he said. "You're embarrassin me. I got a reputation to protect." He went back into the barn. I ran home, wandering through the fields and crying and thinking about the real bad purple bruise I'd seen a while back on Mom's shoulder.

Next day I hitched a ride to Aunt Martha's in Bedford and stayed there till I got into that trade school in Ft. Wayne. Now you know why I didn't come back for Dad's funeral last summer. I was afraid I might embarrass him.

BROTHER

I never got along real well with my little brother. I always figured if his brain didn't need him for transportation, it would have killed him a long time ago. He was like a lightning rod for trouble. Hell, once he even got hit by lightning! But he'd always always shrug it off, put the blame on something else. I'd say, "Bro, if the traffic is coming your way, you're in the wrong lane. Wake up and smell the headlights!" But he'd just give me that spaced-out look and dumb, dopey grin — absolutely clueless. I'd think, how could we even be from the same gene pool?

But we are. Which is why I'm alive right now. When the disease got real bad, they said I needed a bone marrow transplant. He was the only member of my family able — or I should say, willing — to be a donor. I'm alive right now because of my dumb, dopey, absolutely clueless. . . (sobs) I love you, brother. I love you.

ROCK ON

(strums guitar) Powwwwwww! Yeh, rock *on!* Man, my parents keep buggin me about my music. Just cause the songs are all about death and devils and goin crazy and bein insane. And their point is? When I'm not playing music, it's like I ain't even here. I'm a nobody stuck no place goin nowhere, just a big spazoid stumblin around lost in the dark. A ship driftin on the ocean, every day just blow here and there, always about to smash up and sink and drown, but this guitar — it's my anchor.

Sometimes I don't even wanna let go of it. Not to eat, not to sleep, not for nothin. Afraid if I leave it, I'll never find it again. And end up just floatin away.

YOUR BEST FRIEND

Anger is always with me. Always inside me, waiting patiently to be called out. Anger is my best friend. It has never failed me. Never let me down. You laugh? I buried the last cholo laughed at me. *Buried* him! You need my anger, carnal. My anger gonna look out for you. Gonna be there for you when you're in a jam. Respect my anger. Learn from it. Like I respect my father. He beat the crap outa me when I was five years old cause I messed up the laundry, folded the socks inside out or something. I hate him, but I respect him. I respect his anger. His anger showed me my place in the world and where to find the anger in myself. But my anger is better cause I can control it, use it, make it work for me when there is no one else who will stand up and get the job done. Anger is your best friend. And if you are careful, easy, and wise — it will be the only friend you'll ever need.

BREAK-UP CLUES

Relationships can be very mystifying for a teenager. You need to be attuned to every nuance, every subtle hint in the changing fortunes of your romance. For instance, how can you tell when your girlfriend is thinking about breaking up with you? Here's a top ten list of clues:

Clue Number Ten, she shows up for your date even later than usual and says she was abducted by aliens.

Clue Number Nine, she replies to everything you say with the phrase "That's what *you* think."

Clue Number Eight, she starts calling you by your best friend's name.

Clue Number Seven, she asks you what gender you *really* are.

Clue Number Six, she casually remarks that her parents offered her a new car to dump you — and asks if you think gold seats go better with a blue or green dashboard.

Clue Number Five, she asks "But what are you *really* thinking?" every ninety seconds.

Clue Number Four, when you ask to kiss her, she exclaims "But I just brushed my teeth!"

Clue Number Three, when you ask what kind of fierce jungle animal she thinks you resemble, she breaks into hysterical laughter.

Clue Number Two, she starts the conversation with "I have a slight confession to make. . ."

And the Number One Clue your girlfriend is thinking about breaking up with you — you've just finished paying for dinner, and she leaves the going-steady ring you gave her as a tip. And says loudly so the waiter can hear, "Oh, look, this check number is the exact same number as my cell phone!"

Happy romance, kids!

FEMALE or MALE
MONOLOGUES

DESTINY

How did I get this great job working at the Shoe Biz Discount Footwear Emporium? Destiny, that's how! I was walking down Mill Street coming back from recycling the family gar-baje at Grand Union — for which menial task I earn the pathetic sum of five dollaroopos to add to my so-called higher education investment fund — when I saw this piece of paper blow off the windshield of Mrs. Fernbottle's old Plymouth. . . saw it float across the church parking lot, over the sidewalk, spin up almost to the top of the Strand marquee, then down again, then up, then down again, then up and then down zooming past the head of the black-and-white beagle that sits and drools in front of the Yogurt Nook all day. . . and land right on my left shoe print-side up staring me in the face. "Is a Career in Shoes in *Your* Future?" it asked. Whoa!!! Now *that* is destiny! I mean, if it had landed on my arm, I'd be working at some loser place like Sleeve Spa.

ALIEN PLANET

Sure, it's a little scary at times. I mean, what if *you* were suddenly set down in the middle of a hostile alien planet? You didn't speak the language, didn't eat the food, didn't know the customs — and everybody looked at you like you had three heads and they wanted to chop them off *bam-bam-bam!* Talk about stress! Talk about panic! Talk about not knowing if you'll be able to survive one more minute of madness and terror! *(pause)* And, whoa-dang — this is only the *first* day of high school!

WORK WITH IT

(blows softly into a harmonica) Each harmonica you buy is just a little bit out of tune on some notes. My grandpa explained it to me, and it was kinda complicated. Something to do with the "temperament" of the scale, whatever. And if you took it back you'd just get another harmonica that was out of tune, only in a different place. So what do you do with an already out-of-tune harmonica? You work with it. You figure out where it's weak, where it's strong. Which notes you can bend without breaking the tone. Which ones vibrate longer. Which holes are easiest to blow. You try to learn as much as you can from it, while it lasts. I mean, it's just a *thing*. A cheap chunk of metal and plastic that's out of tune the minute it gets made and will never ever be perfect no matter how much you tinker with it. Kinda like people, huh? You take it for what it is. You think about the neat stuff it does — you don't worry about what it doesn't do. Like, when you blow into it *(blows more loudly into harmonica)*, you can feel vibrations against the bones of your skull and sometimes the plastic part your lips touch. It almost feels like it's pulling your whole tongue into where the reeds are, and you can *taste* the sound coming off the metal just as it jumps into the air, and you're jumping *with* it, your entire body riding along as it flies onto the wind, past the trees, over the houses and the whole town, through the clouds all the way into space and the stars and the planets, and all the while you've got this incredible sound zinging in your ears that's, like, from another world! I mean, it can be a hassle, but a harmonica is really, really a trip! So, you work with it. Kinda like people, huh?

A PEOPLE PERSON

When I grow up I'm gonna work in a big office like my dad —
cause he's a people person! Alllllll day long he gets *your* people
to talk to *his* people and *their* people and *everybody's* people.
People put other people on hold to take *his* call, and people
think about *him,* and people wonder about what *he* thinks
about *their* people, and those people tell other people what
they think *he* thinks about their people and about all the other
people who think about *him* all the time because they're *his*
people, or at least they wanna be *his* people so they can think
about *him* and he can think about *them* and they will never-
never-never *not* have people thinking about them, because
when my dad comes home after work. . . he's too tired to think
about me.

FORBIDDEN FRUIT

(reading magazine, then looks up and suddenly closes it and hides behind back) What? Nothing, sir, no, really! *(pause)* All right, you caught me, it's a magazine, do I get detention for possession of contraband wood pulp? Show it to you? *(grimaces)* Come on, it's, I'd rather, do I have to? Okay. *(slowly takes magazine from behind back)* Please, sir, don't tell *anyone*! I'm begging you! If word got out that I was, like, into, you know, this kind of — promise? Oh, thank you! Why? Maybe it's a hunger for knowledge, forbidden fruit. Lately, I just can't stop. I *have* to know. I *have* to know what's happening in the world beyond — beyond this school, beyond this town, beyond MTV and the mall. I'm hooked, addicted, I know I'm risking my reputation! But, please, sir — if my friends ever caught me reading *U.S. News and World Report* —

ASK A SILLY QUESTION

(seated, head bowed) Yes, I know it's wrong to shoplift. Yes, I know it was a very stupid thing to do. No, I don't want to end up like mom. Yes, I want to get into a good college. No, I don't want to get thrown off the soccer team. Yes, I care about our standing in the community. No, I don't want to embarrass you in front of your boss. Yes, I know I hurt you very much. . . *(looks up)* why? Why did I steal the stupid wristwatch? Because for the few hours I was in this jail cell, I didn't have to answer any damn questions from you!

ONE CHANCE A DAY

(ladles out soup, serves coffee) Hi! The nurse comes in at noon, and she'll look at that for you. Sure, have a nice day! *(aside to other person)* My friends ask me why I spend Saturday mornings volunteering at this soup kitchen. I'm not out to save the world, and I am *definitely* not going for a career in social work! I don't even feel that sorry for most of these people — whoa, look at that guy, I think he seriously lives in a sewer. Truth? I do it for my grandmother. She used to tell us stories about the old days when she was growing up. They lived near the railroad, and about once a day a homeless guy would come to her family's back door, a different guy every time. They called them hobos back then, and they'd ask to do chores for money, but grandma didn't have work or money to give, so she'd ask if they were hungry. They always were, and she'd make a sandwich and fill up an empty fruit jar with milk, and the hobos would sit on the back porch and eat and drink and hand back the plate and jar with not a crumb or a drop showing and then move on. I asked my grandmother why she did that, when her own family hardly had any money themselves. She said a hobo could get a handout pretty much any time. But she only had one chance a day to be kind to a stranger the way she'd want someone to be kind to her. "It wasn't for their sake," said my grandmother. "It was for mine."

FOREVER FAMILY

I read about it in the paper. We were in the same foster home when we were ten. I liked him. He smiled a lot and was always happy, no matter how bad things got. And they get real bad sometimes. But Tommy never lost faith. Never lost hope. He never lost trust, and that's the first thing you lose in foster care. First thing I lost, anyway. So when he got adopted by his "forever family" last year, I figured all his trusting paid off. Till I read that his new parents took him on a camping trip, drowned him and made it look like an accident. So they could collect a couple millions bucks in life insurance money they'd took out on their little angel boy. I bet Tommy never knew what hit him. Even if he did, he wouldn't have believed it. He'd have just kept smiling and trusting. I guess they really were his forever family.

OUR TURN TO GIVE

(unfolds a piece of paper, then crumples it) I had some stuff written out to say about Kimberly. About what she meant to her classmates, her friends. But when something this bad happens to someone that good, I don't know what anybody can say that makes any difference. Except. . . except that in her dying — in the really bad way she died — she changed our lives. Kids that never liked each other much, I see them here today in this church, and I see them hugging each other and talking to each other, probably some the first time ever. And if you maybe add up all the good things she did in her short life, all the smiles she gave, all the songs she sang, all the kindness she did. . . well, you hear people say you don't get something for nothing in life, but Kimberly, she gave us all a whole lot of something every day she lived, and she never asked a thing in return. I figure now, we could start giving back.

WICCA IS A RELIGION

(clears throat, nervously shuffles in place) Members of the School Board: I wish to speak against the measure now before you that would ban the wearing of Wiccan symbols of worship at my school. Such as the shiny silver pentagram I myself am now wearing. *(points to neck, clears throat)* Wicca is a religion. And Wiccans are just normal people doing normal things. We do not worship the devil. We do not offer blood sacrifices. We do not eat babies — except on Sundays. Oops, hah-hah, just kidding, I see everybody's awake now! *(clears throat)* I'm not trying to change your ideas about our religion. I'm not even going to try to explain it to you. *(grasps pentagram)* But before you vote, ask yourself this question: f the people who run the schools can take *our* pentagram and make it illegal, why couldn't they do the same with *your* crucifix?

NO ANIMALS WERE HARMED

No animals were harmed in the writing of this monologue. Wish I could say the same about my father and the *huge* rant he went into last night when I happened to mention at dinner — always the worst time to bring up anything meaningful while the family is barking down their slabs of micro-nuked creature flesh — that I was a Vegan. "Those people are fanatics, nut-balls, whackos!" he screams. "They're so confrontational!" Which is slightly sub-ironic, since *he's* the one slamming the table with his fists and making Aunt Marci's chihuahua wet herself on the dining room carpet. My father is mucho empathy-challenged. He thinks Veganism is something invented by liberals to make a parent's life difficult. He sees the animal world as just another *thing* created for his pleasure, like Dockers and the Classic Car Channel and Jodie Foster movies. He's real big on "fitting in" and "not rocking the boat." He could care less if his actions were part of a robo-cop corporate mindset that promotes mass subjugation of native peoples and criminal misuse of irreplaceable planetary resources. *(seethes, then sighs)*

Know what the worst of it is? My father is the master chef at Chez Blanc's. And he makes the best-tasting chicken-fried pork-and-veal crepes in the universe!

THE REVOLUTION WILL NOT BE SUPERSIZED

Hi, my name is Tommy Liz Helmut D or Calvin Estee Fubu, and I'm a charter member of Generation Now On Sale, the good life at a great price, an original classic luxury edition beaucoup de cool at the Gap. The Revolution will not be supersized. What'cha gonna do the dew? The science of you? Got image? Image is nothing. Experience the magic of smooth, see the U.S.A., obey your thirst, just *do* it. The Revolution will not be supersized. Yo quiero joy of cola, drivers wanted, use only as directed, easy open, kids inhale it maximum strength, have it your way, did somebody say multi-functional exercise machine for great sexy abs? No rules, just wrong, don't hold back, can't resist the mist, got milk, got game, got the urge? Feel the tingle, feel the burn, feel the curve, come to where the flavor is, it's a mouthful, the difference is delicious, customize your life, wider is better, it's a woman thing for real men, and that was only the first bite. The Revolution will not be supersized. Think, don't smoke, stop the violence, stop yourself, fire it up, fresh goes better, I know Victoria's dirty little secret and Delia's cover girl, and The Revolution will not be supersized, t will be gel-smooth, ph-balanced, buzzworthy, like a rock, like the core of a breath saver, like a revolutionary new largest-hippest-biggest-baddest-latest new revolutionary new hot pockets Limited as seen on television, order now! The Revolution will *not* be supersized because The Revolution is on sale at www.Our-Kids-Dance-to-the-Pied-Piper-dot-com.

SCIENCE PROJECT

Umm, I won't be handing in a science project today. Yes, I know it's an important part of our grade, but, well, it's been hydro-cuted by the county sheriff's department. Wait, I did not make that word up — "hydro-cuted" is when you execute something by means of water. But I *am* telling the truth! *(sighs)* I was up all night finishing the very last part of the project, and I barely caught the bus this morning. When we got to school, I don't know, I guess I just forgot it on the bus, and it was all wrapped up in a brown box. So when the bus gets back to the garage, the driver finds the box. He freaks and calls the sheriff, and they freak and call the bomb squad, and they freak and bring in the bomb dogs, and they freak and start biting their handlers, so everybody freaks and they haul out this humongous water cannon deal and aim it at the box — which by now I'm trying to get to, but no so-called adults are listening to *me* — and the water cannon blasts the box into a zabillion pieces but then freaks and jumps off *its* axle and blows out five windows in the gym and whips the toupee off Principal Morgan before it runs out of water. And that's why I won't be handing in a science project today. Thank you, please save your applause, thank you.

What *was* the project? Umm, it was a solar-powered worm farm. Eight hundred ribbon worms, all washed down the sewer drain right behind the cafeteria. Never knew what happened to em, poor little squigglers. Umm, I don't know about you, but I'm not ordering spaghetti at lunch today.

I JUST WANT TO KNOW

I want to find my birth parents. But I'm afraid of upsetting my adoptive mom and dad. They're real nice and all, gosh, they've raised me since I was a baby and given me everything I could ever need, including love when lots of times I wasn't very lovable. But I want to see my birth parents cause — no, I don't want to ask why they gave me up. I don't want to be friends with them. I don't even care if we like each other, I just. . . ever feel like you're about one step from being somebody else? Like, if you went around the corner one day, your life might take a swerve, and when you came back around, you'd be someone else, or not quite the person you were before in a major way? I just want to know who I *might* have been. Who I was *supposed* to be until fate stepped up and whisked me away to this other reality. I just want to know. I just. . . gotta know. . .

CONTENT

(typing on computer keyboard) IF YOU CAN'T HANDLE THE CONTENT ON MY WEB SITE — LEAVE. *(looks up)* The content of this site is about nothing. My life is about nothing. My life is a forlorn and desperate attempt to be a beneficial organism in the great compost heap of life. If you are reading this, you're standing too close! You should immediately shut off your computer and get a life. You won't find intelligent life on the Internet, only a twisting labyrinth of endless imaginary pathways leading everywhere, nowhere, elsewhere, upstairs, in the air, unaware, solitaire, double dare, fanfare, Vanity Fair, Smoky the Bear, a millionaire in Delaware driving in his underwear, who cares — see how easy it is to spool off the main thread? *(types)* IF YOU CAN'T HANDLE THE CONTENT OF MY LIFE — *(sighs)* neither can I.

I WANNA BE SURPRISED

When did I know I'd become an Official Teenager? Well, it wasn't the day my voice changed. It wasn't the day I discovered sex. It was when every conversation with my parents became a "talk-to-your-kids-about-the-world" public service announcement. You know what I mean. Every little comment they make ends up as a big Lecture on Life. Last night I'm drying dishes after supper, and my mom starts in on the importance of household chores to developing the proper sense of discipline that makes good study habits in college which will, inevitably and indubitably, lead to a dream job at some microserf cube farm ten years in the future and a house in the suburbs, and it's like, Mo-om! I don't wanna know the future! I wanna be *surprised!* Have it smack me upside the head, mess me around, lead me on, throw me for a loop, knock the wind out of my sails, send me flying! I know you want to help me protect me, share your hard-earned wisdom. But don't take away the surprise. That's the best thing about growing up — not knowing how anything's gonna turn out. And when you can't be surprised anymore, I don't think you're even very much alive.

WHO'S KEEPING SCORE, MOM?

Report cards came today. I had five A's and one B. First thing my mother says? "What did you get the B in?" Hmmm, let's see, mom, is it my imagination, or do my failures attract more attention than my successes? Cause, it's always that way with her. I sort out five piles of laundry, one pair of socks is mismatched, it's major conversation for the next week. What about the other fifty pairs of correctly matched socks? They don't exist? I mean, who's keeping score, mom? Who's handing out the prize for Total Perfection? Is God keeping track in some big balance book of everything I do? Ten mismatched pair of socks equals a mortal sin equals three extra months in Purgatory?

When I do something right, be proud of me. Or maybe I'll just quit bothering to do anything right at all.

BROTHER'S KEEPER

My younger brother is out of control, totally off the hinges, buggin! So who's the one gets yelled at? Me ! My parents say I'm supposed to be a good influence, a role model. Okay, *I* don't lie or steal or set stuff on fire, but when *he* does, it's somehow *my* fault? *My* responsibility? When did *I* get elected family behavior cop? I thought that was the parents' job. I am *not* my brother's keeper. I can't control him any more than they can. They should put him in a zoo with the other animals. And charge admission to go to my college fund.

ANY SECOND NOW

First thing my dad does when he sits down in the living room is grab the channel changer. He *has* to find it, *has* to seize it, has to *control* it — even if we're in the middle of a show I'm watching, even if the TV isn't on. He doesn't do anything with it at first, just holds it awhile. Then, slowly, shifts it between one hand and the other. Then starts to finger it. You can hear the rustling noise — *swip-swip!* — flesh on rubber, and the *creeaak-creeaak!* of the plastic, as he squeezes his thumb down on the side, at this point you're completely distracted from whatever you were doing — *huth-huth!* — he's breathing harder now, almost hyperventilating *huth-huth!* gonna make his move *swip-swip! huth-huth!*, any second now, he's gonna punch-and-go, punch-and-go, it's like having a gun pointed next to your head, *swip-swip! huth-huth! swip-swip! huth-huth! creeeeaaak!* the pressure builds until you want to scream!

That's when I leave the room. And he wonders why we don't spend any time together as a family. Jeez, I'd rather be given Chinese water torture. At least you know when that next drop is gonna hit!

AN OLD BOX OF TAPES

After the divorce went through, I was helping load my dad's stuff into the van. I found a box of old music tapes from when he was in college. One of them had a song on it called "Can We Still Be Friends?" by some hermit guy in Mink Hollow or wherever. I took the tape, and that night, I listened to it. It was a good song, even though it was from, like, the '70s. I listen to that song a lot, in secret sort of. And I think about how some time when mom and I visit dad, maybe I'll play that tape for them. . . play that song. And when they hear it, they'll look at each other, and they'll remember the good times they had when they first heard it, cause once upon a time it must have meant something major to them, and then they'll, well, maybe they'll think about — I don't know. I mean, I can't see how two people can just fall out of love and leave each other behind, like an old box of tapes.

RÉSUMÉ

(filling out application) Let's see. Previous job experience and outcomes. Outcomes, hmmm. . . two months phone sales associate for Frank's Furniture Warehouse — *(writes)* "aided customers in piling up huge, crushing debt". . . six weeks stock clerk Midtown Auto Supply — *(writes)* "improved local air quality by re-routing shipment of truck parts to Buenos Aires". . . three weeks service rep Psycho-Tech Software — *(writes)* "developed free-range email virus to assist clients in reducing Internet dependence". . . two days prep cook Sandy's Snack Shack — *(writes)* "helped diners appreciate value of home cooking". . . *(raises hand)* Excuse me, does "salmonella" have one or two *N*'s?

I PROMISE I'LL BE DEEP

(looks up surprised) Ayo? I'm sorry, teacher. Nuh-uh, wasn't *takin* nothin! I was puttin my cable in your desk. *In* your desk. Say what? Cable cost me buck money, pure gold, see? Don't want no bootsy chumpin it. Put it in my locker? Don't have no locker. Oh, *that* locker? Nobody give me my lock! Say what? Have to buy my own? Whassup with that? Whoo, had a lock but lost it. Nuh-uh, had a lock, forgot the combo. Some lick trim it anyway, what good's a lock in this ville? Listen, teach, be a cuz and let me park my rope and you just clock it for me till school's out. You do, I promise I'll be deep in class today. Deep and low down. Dead up!

MOM, I LOVE YOU

Mom? It wasn't your fault Dad left, and nobody thinks it was. I'm glad I'm living with you, I really am, but. . . but every night you just go in the den and you just. . . I hate seeing you like that, I hate seeing you get sick all the time, I hate seeing you act like no one cares cause they do. *I* do. You think I'm just a kid and can't know how a grown-up feels, but I haven't spent my whole childhood watching cartoons! I can see real things going on, and — and I think, well, I know you're really sad and. . . Mom, I love you. But I wish you'd quit drinking. Will you? Tonight? Please?

BRIDGE KIDS

They call us Bridge Kids, cause we hang out on the bridge over the canal. And cause we're pretty much always here, in the day when the touristas wander by in search of exotic locals, and at night when the party people flock to the bars. We're not "homeless," okay? The Bridge is our home. It's our community. It's our office, hey, got any spare change? Thanks. Bridge Kids take care of each other. Couple days ago Randy's old man came here with a cop, but there's no way Randy's going back home to get whomped on anymore, so we hid him out till they gave up and left. Sure we look spiky. We want you to keep your distance, okay? Go ahead laugh at us and feel sorry for us. Hell, you can take our pictures all day, sell them to the newspaper, whatever. Just don't get too close. The Bridge can hold only so much weight. Keep moving and don't worry about what's underneath.

MORE JUST OKAY

I look around, and I don't see very much Happy. Happy is largely absent from this sphere of existence. Who do *you* know who's really Happy? My parents aren't. My brother and sister aren't. My friends aren't, and neither are any kids I see in school. Teachers, no way. Can you even say a dog or butterfly is truly Happy? People in the supermarket, the mall, on the streets, even at church, none of them are Happy, so I don't think it's just a teen thing, a "phase."

And the more people tell you to *be* Happy, the more un-Happy you get. That's like a Law of Perverse Mental Physics, cause if you really believe Happy is the natural way of things, and you're *not* insanely and berserkly Happy, you get more depressed and miserable till you're drowning in a swamp of wanna-be-Happy but can't because your emotional dipstick is stuck in the mud at the shallow end of the gene pool.

So, maybe everybody should stop working so hard to be Happy. Maybe they should think about being more Just Okay. In fact, I think Happy is way too much to ask of anybody, especially people who are hopelessly cruel and greedy and always starting wars and dumb trading card fads. From now on, I want the world to be Just Okay. Less Happy, more Just Okay.

Wouldn't that make you Happy?

WE TAG, WE TESTIFY

Yo, dog, I'm a mad bomber and tonight this town is gonna burn! Oh, right, I gotta talk "mainstream" to you. A "bomber" is what *you* call a quote-unquote graffiti artist. And "burn" means me and my crew are gonna bring some living color to this black-and-white cartoon of a city. So, relax, dog — our deadly weapons are air and paint. *(mimes spraying)* *Whoosh!*

Why? Cause this is *my* world, too, and I'm gonna make it come alive! Make it rise up and speak in a new way, every day. Gonna give it brightness, definition, perspective, uh-huh, I went to art school, too. See that overpass? Blank concrete, straight dull, that overpass is a *crime* — Crime of Style! Yo, how many homes you think got torn down for that overpass? How many people's lives got ripped apart when the city kicked em outa their house and ran em off into the sunset? Tearing down a family's home for a damn concrete overpass, that's serious vandalism, dog. Serious disrespect. Me and my crew, we're on a mission. Every time we tag, we testify for the ghosts.

JUST PERFECT

(writing in notebook) ". . . takes one step to the left and—" *(looks up)* Hi! Yeh, another list. Almost got it right this time. Jesse starts off with a song, "Hearts upon the Wind." Make sure there's a keyboard for backup. Then Shondra reads two of my poems — *Incombustible* and *Frequent Fencing*— and then the quote from Lil Kim about true love being like mayonnaise. Shondra steps back, and from the right side comes Tony and Marcus and Jean, and from left Danesha, Maria, and Lynn, each holding a bouquet of these real neat pink flowers called Autumn Joy. Which they lay on the altar, as Jesse — who should be wearing a grey cape and silver gloves — leads everyone out with "Never Cry for Twilight."

(turns the page) My mom says it's weird to plan your own funeral, when you're only twelve. But she doesn't know what it's like to be twelve years old in this neighborhood. When my time comes, I want everything to be just perfect.

EMERGENCY FLORADECTOMY

(on knees digging in the dirt with a trowel) This is my favorite place in the whole world. Since I was, like, four years old, all us kids in the subdivision spent every chance we got running around out here in the woods. Catching frogs, playing jungle hunt, looking for snakes, wading through the creek and imagining we were explorers in Africa or Asia or some alien planet or maybe even millions of years back in time with a T-Rex lurking behind those big twisty vines. Or sometimes just sitting on a rock and listening to all the wood sounds and watching sunbeams filter through the trees and dance and wave and scatter along the ground in really neat shapes.

(looks to right) Tomorrow that steam shovel's gonna start tearing down the woods. Our woods all of it. I guess having a new video store and drug store and pizza place close by is okay. But I got my own little shovel, and I'm taking some creek stuff back to plant in our yard. Got a little tulip poplar here. And a trumpet vine would look cool on the patio wall. This salamander egg, I'm gonna take to school for a science project. Hey, maybe it's really a dinosaur egg, and it'll hatch and grow up and devour the new strip mall! *(chuckles, sighs)* I'm gonna miss these woods.

ALPHABET SOUP

HIV. STD. HPV. DNA. FAQ. ATM. MTV. BET. ADD. AD*H*D. . . CPU-RAM-WWW-dot-CNN-GTE-UPS-AOL-APR-GNP-DVD-LSD. *(gasps for breath)* Better get on it PDQ-COD-FYI-TCB-ASAP-NIMBY! Look out, it's the CIA-NRA-IRS-AKA that SOB, IMHO — look, a UFO! Heard the new LFO on MP3? RSVP your ETA BYO. I need some ESP on the SAT to get my MBA and be a CEO-DDS-PHD or I am SOL! Can you please pass the MSG before the next Y3K TBA following the NFL-NBA on NBC. *(waves good-bye)* English language, RIP!

CURFEW

(stands with hands outstretched, fists closed, palms down)
Where's the fire? Officer, I respectfully request you tell me the location of the fire. *(handcuffs snap on, hands drop)* You're arresting us for curfew violation, right? So, being the intelligent, well-trained law enforcement professional you are, you obviously know that our word "curfew" is derived from the medieval French *covrefeu*, which was the bell rung in the town square that meant you had to put out the fire in your hearth. So, if there's no fire, officer, how can there be a curfew? Excuse me? Hearth — it's like a fireplace, same thing, different word, don't they have crossword puzzles lying around the donut shop? Yes, sir, I do. I always talk like this. Why do you think my parents locked me out of the house?

COLORING IT IN

(on knees, drawing and rubbing with chalk on pavement) I don't really think of myself as an artist. Not by choice, anyway. I really don't *want* to be on my knees in the cold right now, and I'm not very good at it, either. But when your best friend gets blown away in a parking lot for no good reason, what else you gonna do? Some people came and prayed awhile yesterday, and I saw that where the police made the outline of his body, the chalk was already starting to fade. That outline, it's the last piece of him the world will ever see. So I'm coloring it in, and maybe people will walk by and notice it and, I dunno, *do* something. I don't really think of myself as an artist. I just don't like thinking anybody's life can disappear like chalk on the pavement.

GOOD JOB TRAINING

(typing on computer keyboard) Danc! Froze up again! Well, that's what happens when you got a computer from the Stone Age. Our school is one of those pocr, olc, inner-city schools everybody feels sorry for — and afraid of. So we get a lot of free stuff to pacify the natives and ease the school board's conscience. Pre-owned videos, pencils with the erasers worn off, desks with different-size legs, used textbocks with the wrong answers already filled in, computers that don't work cause you can't get parts anymore. I guess they're really just using us for a garbage dump. But, hey, this is good job training. I was thinking about going into a career in recycling, anyway.

HOME ALONE

If my parents had their way, I would never be alone for one second of my life. Like tonight, they're getting a babysitter while they go out for two hours! What are they afraid can happen in two hours of me being home alone? I'm going to be knifed by a maniac? Kidnapped by a cult? Struck dead by a meteor that just happens to hit *our* living room? Or maybe invite a friend over and do something dangerous, like leave the icemaker in the "up" position? It's like they won't stop seeing me as anything but a little kid who has to be watched every minute or I fall down go boom hurt myself owww! I wish they'd realize there's going to be a lot of times coming up where I fall down and go boom. I'm ready for it, why aren't they?

DIFFERENT DREAMS

I know you had dreams, dad. Once upon a time, back in the day. Grammom said you were pretty heavy into your training for a long time, and things looked good for awhile. But I'm not you. And I have different dreams. Dreams I'm just starting to know about, just starting to even realize exist. My dreams are just as important to me as yours were to you. And maybe I'll make them come true, maybe not. But I have to try, the same way you tried. I just wish you could support me in my dreams, instead of always making me feel bad cause I'm not living up to yours.

ASPIRATIONS

Uh-huh, this is my first time to see a guidance counselor. Yeh, I'm a senior, gonna graduate next week. I hope! *(crosses fingers, chuckles)* Do I have "aspirations"? Yeh, sure, ummm, according to my dad, I'm gonna be a minimum wage worker and then maybe graduate to being a paid test subject for medical experiments. Uh-huh, he's always been real supportive of our aspirations. He told my sister she was gonna be a welfare queen and have three kids before she was twenty, and dang if he wasn't right! Huh? What kinda career do I *really* want? Ummm, I didn't know I got to choose. Do I have to choose right now? Do I get punished if I choose the wrong answer? There isn't any wrong answer? You sure? My dad always says life is one big test, and if you study hard and fail, you're a bigger dummy than if you didn't learn anything to start with. And he oughta know. *(spits to the side)* He's the biggest dummy I've ever seen, and he learned it all on his own.

PARENTAL LOGIC

Parents will be parents will be parents. (chuckles) How many times have you heard that before? They're so predictable, so easy to woof. Yesterday, I got back from the mall, had a fake stick-on tongue stud. (sticks out tongue) Parents go ballistic. (in parents' voice) "You'll never wear that as long as you live in this house! Do you know the diseases you can get? You look like a circus freak! Where's your self-respect?" Etcetera and so forth and yabba-dabba-boo-wow. I calmly remove the offending faux-accessory, and they get even *more* berserk. Because now, I've *deceived* them. And *I'm* at fault because I didn't do what they thought I did. (sighs) Parental logic — an oxymoron if there ever was one.

ARE YOU TRULY DEPRESSED?

Hey, there, American Teenagers! Want to know if you're *truly* depressed? Here's an easy 10-point quiz. Do you:

One, feel tired all the time and have no energy — except for devouring a 36-inch pizza between meals?

Two, feel sad or cry a lot — like whenever your parents insist on accompanying you and your friends to the mall to help you "pick out a few duds"?

Three, feel restless and morose during school — especially when your teacher is droning on about the Hawley-Smoot Trade Tariff Act of 1930 and its ramifications on your weekly allowance.

Four, think life is meaningless and nothing good is ever going to happen again — because your favorite music group broke up and you just spent your entire life savings wallpapering your room with hundreds of their photos.

Five, have a negative attitude a lot of the time, or have no feelings at all — ever since that totally fly hotty you just *knew* was crazy for you went out with your ex-best friend instead.

Six, feel guilty for no reason — because you don't know if that really-really-*really* nasty E-mail message you wrote about you-know-who accidentally got copied to the entire school address list.

Seven, don't feel like doing a lot of the things you used to — because with your new super-beast, type-hot, triple-bomb, phat-dope teenage persona, they make you look even more like the lame-wack-crusty-puddin-whammy-wingnut you secretly believe yourself to be. . . even if you knew what most of those words actually meant.

Eight, forget things and find it hard to concentrate or to

make decisions — because tonight is the final season-ending episode of *Buffy the Vampire Slayer*.

Nine, are irritated often and find that little things make you lose your temper — like being asked by complete strangers to take a meaningless 10-point quiz.

And Number Ten, do you think about death, or feel like you're dying, or have thoughts about committing suicide — because your parents have suddenly shown up at the party you're giving, while they were *supposed* to be away for the *whole* weekend.

Well, if you scored a perfect 10, I have serious news for you, Mr.-slash-Ms. American Teen. *You* are seriously normal! Bummer! Now, go on, get a life! Or charge one to your parents' credit card!

THE WAY COLLEGE IS SUPPOSED TO BE

If I went to college, I'd be the first one in my family to ever do it. Which is cool. But kinda weird. I mean, it's not like my parents are putting pressure on me one way or the other, but — I don't know. I don't know if I can handle college. And if I don't, I mean, what if I screw up and can't cut it and have to bail? Sure I'm as smart as the kids I know who are going, and I had a good SAT score, and State offered me a scholarship, but what if — what if college isn't, you know, for me? Will people think I'm a loser? That I let my family down? Will I just, you know, make things worse for everybody? Instead of better, the way college is supposed to be.

SLEEP!

(yawns groggily, then jerks awake, mumbling) Uhhh, a bucket of geraniums added to one quart Philadelphia cream cheese defeated Rutherford B. Hayes in the First Crusade! *(blinks rapidly)* Oh, wow! No, I'm wide awake, sir, wide awake! What was the question? The atomic weight of vanadium, I'm sorry, no, I haven't been getting enough sleep, I-I-I will, sir. *(to student at right)* Say, how do *you* keep awake in this boring class? I read in a magazine the other day that teenagers need at least nine hours sleep a night, but that because our hormones are changing so rapidly, we can't actually fall asleep till before, like, almost midnight. Word! Then we're forced to get up at the crack of dawn to get to school by the ridiculous hour of 9 A.M.? Huh? School starts at 7:15? Oops! Then the whole deadly sleep deprivation cycle starts all over, every day! It's not fair! We're hamsters on a mill! I mean, really, sometimes, adults blame everything on *(yawns)* on us kids. . . *(frowns, nods)* I could just *(yawns)*. . . mmmmm. . . *(falls asleep, then jerks awake, mumbling)* Grasshopper said to the Oldsmobile: "Mister, I don't think the square root of one hundred fourteen plus thirty-nine thousand bazillion has anything to do with the perfume I'm smelling on your porcupine." *(blinks rapidly)* Oh, wow!

DOUBLE LIFE

I have a very, very deep, dark secret. I am not an ordinary teenager. I lead a double life. I perform. . . in an ethnic dance troupe.

Ssshhh! I don't want anybody at school to find out! People would think I was, you know, *moist*. But my parents started me on it when I was six years old. I hated it at first. All that hopping around, and the yerpy costumes, and the bizarro music with the twangy-bangy instruments. Like, no wonder people left the Old Country! *(chuckles)* Then, I don't know, at some point, I started to like it. I found I could dance really well, which is cool, and I picked up some awesome body moves that impress my school buds. And it was fun being part of a team. Fun being part of a show. Fun making people clap and laugh and shout and think of the good times in their life. Think of their home and family and friends and just feel good about themselves in a way they can't always express now that they live here. But we can express it for them. And we can still be Americans.

YOUR HOROSCOPE FOR TODAY

And here's your personalized teen horoscope for today:

Aries — you'll feel the effects of the moon circling the sun and piggybacking Venus as it sideswipes Jupiter in a double-tectonic macarena with North Dakota. Stay inside and lock the doors!

Taurus has romance on the brain all day, as a harmonic convergence of planets in your forty-ninth house makes you yearn for a one-on-one partnership with your long-sought soul mate. Too bad! They're already taken!

Gemini will enjoy a calm, average, blissfully mellow day. Actually, you'll be so insanely bored, you'll resort to watching paint dry on dead bugs for excitement.

For **Cancer**, the day starts off on a positive note as the moon transits your sign and renders you more psychic and sensitive than usual to the inner vibrations of others. And, yes, everyone is secretly laughing at your silly haircut.

The moon enters **Leo's** sun sign on Tuesday. On Wednesday, the sun enters Leo's moon sign. On Thursday, the moon tells the sun to get lost, because Leo only has room for one celestial body at a time, buster, and by Friday, Leo's sun and moon are brawling like drunken sailors, causing members of this sign to go stark raving bonkers through the weekend.

Virgos will have their fondest wish come true. They just won't remember what it was, and so will continue to be their usual brooding and scatterbrained insufferable selves.

For **Libra**, this week finds you in high demand by friends and family members. Keep your ATM card under lock and key.

Today is a special, special day for **Scorpio**. A thrilling new vista of boundless opportunity will emerge, as you realize for the first time you've been reading the wrong horoscope all these years. You're a scorpion not a crab, dummy!

Sagittarians are free spirits by nature, and tonight you'll want to go with the flow, soar like an eagle, fly your freak flag high! Just remember to tell the nice policeman the devil made you do it and memorize the emergency pager number of your parents' lawyer before you leave the house.

Capricorn's ruling planet, Mercury, enters on Sunday, which means that you'll be super creative and communicative. In fact, it will be virtually impossible to shut you up for the next few weeks, you'll just keep bubbling over with creativity and imagination, pumping out idea after idea after idea after stupid stinking idiotic idea until someone finally puts you out of their misery with a solid blow to the midsection.

Aquarius — be prepared for confusion and difficulty as Neptune goes retrograde in your sign and gives you the biggest, baddest cosmic wedgie in human history. Buy extra insurance within the next twenty minutes. Do it! Now!

And for **Pisces**, Neptune goes retrograde in Aquarius on Monday after the tea harvest fails in Afghanistan. No one really knows what this means, but you should always expect the worst. Odds are it'll cause you to break out in a hideous rash and deplete your brain of at least thirty percent of its operating capacity.

Have a nice day!

FAMILY LIFE

Thanks for coming over, you wanna watch TV? We have TVs in every room of the house, check it out! Dad watches his sports programs in the den. Mom watches her cooking programs in the kitchen. Each of us kids has a TV in our room, and there's a TV in the basement for video games and another in the living room for the satellite dish. When I go by my parents' room at night, that TV is on, even after they're asleep. I saw somebody on the news the other night saying how TV had split up family life and kept everybody in the family isolated from one another, each in their own little private world. I think they're right. And with this family, that's probably a real good thing.

WEATHER REPORT

Today's weather report:

Black clouds looming on the horizon, no silver linings. Cold front arriving with one hundred and ten percent chance of snow mixed with hail, frost, and subzero arctic temperatures, spawning severe tornadic disturbances in upper and lower atmospheres along with life-threatening earthquakes, monsoons, and dislocation of the Earth's orbital axis. Pack an umbrella and a ticket on Noah's Ark.

Following this morning's math test, look for sunshine mixed with periods of unseasonable warmth and rainbows everywhere!

CROSSED SIGNALS

(talking on cell phone) Really? That's unbelievable! No way! Way no way! No way way! No way way no way! Hold on, I've got another call, probably my mom. She bought me this phone for emergencies only. Yeh, right! And elephants fly out my nasal passages! Hang on, I'll be right back. (punches button on phone) Reeking! Wassup, girl! I was just talking to Amanda, and yeh, *she* said that *he* said — oops, pager. (takes pager from belt, speaks into phone) Hey, I just got a hit from my Sugar Slurp network pager! Every day they send a page about a promotion or sometimes just an ad about a new candy bar. Call back right away and you can win a special prize! Hold on! (dials number on phone) Hello! Yes, I want to win a free trip to the Sugar Slurp Slamfest in Sheboygan! Yes, I'll hold! Whoops! (digs in jacket, pulls out pager) My dad's office pager! How did it get in here? (dials number on phone) Hello, umm, he's not here right now, this is his receptionist — who is this? Danny! How did you get dad's pager number? Get off the phone, I'm in the middle of an important contest! (punches button on phone) Hello, Sugar Slurp Contest Line! Oh, Amanda, yeh, that was Kimberly! Sorry, can't talk, I'm in the middle — (punches button on phone) Yes, Sugar Slurp, it's me, I'm ready for the question! The name of the actor who played the robot sidekick in — (grabs at jacket) No! I mean, yes, wait, I know the answer, hold on! (digs in jacket, pulls out another pager) I can't remember what this pager is! (drops pager, punches button on phone) No, you've got the wrong number! (punches button on phone) Sugar Slurp? Dad! I've got your pager, sorry-can't-talk-love-you-bye! (punches button on phone) Hey, I'm back! What? I can't hear you, the signal's weak — (punches button on phone) Hello? Amanda? Kimberly! Can't-talk-bye! (punches button on *phone)* Hello! Get off the phone, Danny! *(punches button on phone)* Mom! No, I don't know where Danny put the — *(punches button on phone)* Yes, the name of the actor who played the robot sidekick is — hello? Hello, Sugar Slurp Contest Line! Hello? *(punches button on phone)* Hello-ooooo! *(punches button on phone)* Hello-hello-hello! *(punches buttons on phone)* They hung up! All of them! Some people have no manners!

THEY NEVER WAVE

I really envy my friends, Jamie and Tanya. They'd laugh to hear that, cause they're both on scholarship at school, and my mom makes more in a week than their whole family makes in a year. But Jamie and Tanya live in the city, in a real neighborhood. They have a little drugstore and a pizza place down the block. A park on the corner to hang out at and watch the world go by. Me? I live in this huge mansion at the end of a cul-de-sac in the middle of a suburb that is five miles by car from *anything*. You have to schedule "appointments" with your friends so your parents can drive you back and forth like chauffeurs or maybe just drop you off at the mall. Nobody ever walks, except on the jogging trail, which you have to drive to cause it's six miles away across the interstate loop. You never see anyone outside, except little kids who ride tricycles in their driveway. Sometimes you get real lonely and run out the front door and just head off in any direction and walk around the subdivision, and you get these real weird looks from people driving by, like you're doing something suspicious. Sometimes you catch a glimpse of somebody in their house peeping out, watching till you pass by. They never wave. Funny, isn't it? There's not much crime out here in suburbia. But there sure is a lot of fear.

ANOTHER CHANCE

Look, try to be grown-up about it. Tell your mom and dad that you'd never tried alcohol before and you just wanted to see what would happen. Parents are soft on the "experiment" thing. Then say it wasn't at all like you expected and that you never want to do it again. That zings their protective button. Tell them the few hours of quote-unquote fun weren't worth the consequences and you feel disappointed in yourself for making a bad choice. Never let them think you enjoyed it. Finally, ask if they can find it in their hearts to forgive you and let you have another chance to prove you're a responsible young adult. They'll be touched by your maturity and go to bed feeling they've done their parental duty. *(takes a long slug from liquor bottle)* Aaah! Then, slip out the back and meet me at the corner. I've got a twelve-pack and a bottle of Jack Black ready to rip!

JOB SECURITY

(leafing through a paperback book) For a summer job, this is pretty cool. Service rep takes a phone order from the catalogue, I pull it, bring it up front, then go back to wait for the next order. Good money, gives me a lot of time to read. No, I don't hang out much with the other clerks. My second day we were all in the lunchroom, and I was reading this book, *On the Road*, about a guy hitching across the country and having all kinds of wild adventures. My boss says, "Hey, you in summer school?" I said, "No," and he says, "Then you must be in J.O.E.," — which stands for Juvenile Offender Education — and I said, "No." And he says, "What you got that book for, then?" "I just like to read," I said, and everybody laughed and went back to talking about some new TV show giving away ten million dollars to whoever can stay the longest on a desert island. Awhile later, it came to me that for him and the others, the only time you read is when somebody *makes* you. Reading is a punishment. It's the last thing you'd *ever* do on your own. *(earmarks book, closes it)* I'll bet you a quarter everybody at this warehouse is working here ten years from now. *(holds up book)* Except for me.

PRIME PARTY TIME

He sat next to me in study hall. He never seemed mad at anybody, or like he was having problems at home. In fact, it seemed like he laughed a lot and was pretty stoked. Didn't say much, though. Guess I never had anything much to say to him, either, or any urge to get deep into his dibs. Then, *boom!* He brings in his old man's rifle and blows all those kids away. Off the hinges!

Course, everybody understands why he *wanted* to kill people. He wouldn't be *normal* if he didn't want to kill *some*body. Just, nobody can understand why he actually put all the effort into *doing* it. That seems like a serious waste of prime party time. I mean, you only get to be a teenager once. Who wants to spend it jerking around with cops and lawyers and other clueless grown-ups?

TRIBES

Let's see, which will it be this time? Stoner? Surfer? Beemer? Goth? Maybe I should get some old-time religion and join the Christians — shout hallelujah! My dad's business takes us to a new town about every eighteen months. This is, like, my thirty-second school, and I'm not even out of eighth grade. What usually works is to make friends with the most nonthreatening people and stay in the background, stay out of the way. But that's harder to do the older you get. *Everybody's* threatening, and you need backup to keep from getting hassled. They don't let you be in the background, everybody's got to be in the show. Let's see, juicers? Jocks? Gangstas? Alfalfas? Hippies? Geeks? Bowheads? Preps? I'm flexible! They're all the same, really. Little tribes with their own little rites, their own dress codes and talk, their own dirty little secrets they gossip about and try to hide from the other cliques. My dad always asks me, what did you learn in school today? *(shrugs)* Basically, to survive.

CONVERSATION PARTNER

Listen, there is no way I am going to a shrink. Why? Because talking to myself is perfectly healthy! I mean, it's not like I'm some loony-tune stumbling around the gutter raving about CIA black helicopters giving him orders through his contact lenses. I just enjoy conversing with myself, I don't care if people hear me, I'm just minding my own business, talking to myself. It passes the time, keeps me focused. And I'm an interesting person. Sort of. Sometimes. Mostly. Well, I'm always interesting when I talk to myself, because I can respond intelligently to what I just said, since I just heard myself say it and knew I was saying it, in fact, knew I was going to say it and knew what I was going to say after hearing it, because I'd just said it and heard myself say it because I was talking to myself, which is no big deal really even out loud like now I'm just talking to myself in a basic conversation which is cool because I'm the one having the conversation with myself and I like it!

Pardon? Yes, please, I'll have another double mocha espresso with a twist of ginseng and dash of kava-kava. Can you put it on our tab?

PAY ATTENTION

Seek professional help if your teenager experiences serious mood changes that last more than a couple of weeks. Seek professional help if your teen says they are thinking about suicide. Be suspicious if they withdraw from family and friends, lose interest in favorite activities, emit expressions of excessive guilt or hopelessness, engage in self-destructive behavior such as drinking, drug abuse, reckless driving, and promiscuity. Pay attention to phrases such as, "It's no use, I'd be better off dead." or "You can have it, I won't be needing it anymore." And, finally, mom and dad — when your teenager wears the key to the gun closet on a chain around their neck for three days in a row and you don't notice or choose to say a word. . . *(grasps neck chain)* you can pretty much kiss that Parent-of-the-Year Award good-bye.

SCOFFIN CHEDDAR
FROM THE RENTS

Hey, shorties, here's a mad piece on scoffin cheddar from the rents. Oh, sorry, I see we have some delegates from Planet Wankoid in the audience, allow me to translate: Here's a quick tutorial on "Tips for Borrowing Money from Your Parents."

One, find out when they get paid. Usually it's the first or the fifteenth of the month, and they're feeling flush and sassy when they see that bank balance rise up from zeroville. Course, it's gonna tank right away soon as they start paying bills, so ask quick before their false euphoria wears off and rationality returns.

Two, asking for cash for your own needs will be successful about one time in ten. You can increase the odds by being selective about what you ask for. For instance, tell dad you wanna buy something nice for mom. *Ka-ching!* You'll get your green and be able to keep significant change from the trinket you purchase. This sometimes works with mom, but not as well since women don't give presents from guilt the way guys do. No matter how totally desperate you are, *never* — I repeat, *never* — tell them you want to buy something for your brother or sister. They'll send you to a shrink and have you drug-tested for hallucinogens every hour.

Three, if you're going out on a date, don't just blurt out your request for cash. Be subtle. Ask them about advice on dating and pretend to listen. Ask them if there was ever a time when they wanted to date but couldn't because they didn't have the grip. Ask them if that made them feel depressed and unpopular, even — dum-de-dum-dum. . . *suicidal*. One hint of the Magic Scary S-Word, and you'll see that ATM card fly out of their wallet!

Four, when your parents ask how much money you have, be honest. Tell them you have a substantial amount in your savings, but it's for college and you don't want to touch it till then. Make sure you actually *have* a savings account before you try this. And if you're currently *in* college, tell them your money's tied up in an offshore retirement fund.

Five, when you get back, give them a little change, no matter how miniscule. It assures them that you're not a complete wastrel and that you have some degree of responsibility. Caution: Do not include lottery tickets, casino chips, beer bottle caps or discount coupons to Psycho Red's Tattoo Parlor in your change.

And finally, remember that your parents work really hard for their money. Taking it away should be as painless as possible. After all, you don't want them to get discouraged. They might quit working and start borrowing from you!

JUST INQUISITIVE

(filing fingernails with nail file) Hi, I'm DSHS. *(chuckles)* No, that's not my name, it's the special scientific term for my disorder. Deliberate Self-Harm Syndrome. I just call it cutting. They say it's about anger, but not with me it isn't. I'm not angry. Just inquisitive. I want to know who I really am. What's underneath my skin — literally. I had a friend who cut to experience pain for the excitement of feeling alive. And they say some of us cut to see our blood flow, to punish ourselves. Not me. I'm a happy person. Everyone says so. I've always been really good at making people feel happy. Pleasing them. Giving them what they want. Being who they want me to be. But not any more. This, this *creature* I see in the mirror isn't the real me. The *real* me is inside, trapped in this skin, and it's time to come out. Inch by inch. Piece by piece. Cut by cut. *(holds up file)* My therapist says self-awareness begins with self-knowledge. I say, if you really want to know who you are, start digging. *(grips file, stares at it, turns it inward)*

GETTING INKED

(seated, rolls up sleeve to shoulder) Yeh, I'm ready for a tattoo — oops, sorry, "skin illustration." Are my buds gonna be amazed when they see I got inked over Spring Break! (points to wall) I'll take that one! I was born the Year of the Dragon, and that is a totally awesome dragon! (squints) It's a sand crab? Would anybody but you and me know the difference? I think the dragon is outside my price range. Uhh, yen, "good tattoos do not come cheap, and cheap tattoos are not good," yeh, I totally copy where you're coming from, man. That's deep. Do I know if I'm a bleeder? Uhh, does that make a difference? Those needles, yeh, the ones from the ashtray, would you mind running a little hot water over the tips? You know what they say, a warm needle is a good needle! (chuckles) Wow, is that your diploma? (points to wall) Oh, I see. The Board of Health wouldn't actually shut you down in the middle of a session, would they? I mean you've probably had years of training and learned from a master artist — Internet correspondence course? Awesome, yeh, uhh, what's that you say? "You get the tattoo you deserve." (rises) Uhh, you know, man, I just remembered fresh ink gives me asthma, and I left my epidermal sequencer device back at the motel, I think I'll just, uhh, maybe step out and wait till I can afford a real dragon. (exits in a rush)

LAW OF THE LAND

(shouting) I don't care! I don't care what they did in the Old Country! This is America, mom, and you can't just buy somebody for me to marry! I know, I know, I've heard the story a million times, you and dad never saw each other before your wedding day, but this is the 21st century and people do *not* marry someone their parents pick out from a book! Respect for the family? What about respect for *me*? They have something in this country, mom, called *pursuit of happiness*. It's like the law of the land, and marrying someone because you love them is your inalienable right no one can take away from you, even your parents. Someday I'm going to meet the person that's right for me, and I have no idea whether they'll be one of *us* or any of the other three thousand types of human beings on this planet. You have to give me that chance, mom. It's the law of the land.

JUST FOR ONCE

(shouting, fists clenched, total tantrum) I will not! I will not! I will *not* stay home and babysit my stupid sister! I'm going to the party! Am so! You can't make me do anything! Disruptive? I'll show you disruptive! (picks up book, throws it on floor) And what're you gonna do if I don't? (slams door, buries face in hands, looks up, anguished) She's quit even trying. It's like there's nothing I do that will get her to pay attention. . . I don't want to go that damn party. I want — just for once. . . just for once, mom, I want you to say no!

THIS IS YOUR BRAIN ON MORTAL KOMBAT

(reading from magazine) "The latest versions of Doom, Mortal Kombat and Half Life feature realistic depictions and sounds of violence that are close to motion-picture quality, as limbs are blown off and organs splattered. Experts say these video games teach children to connect glory and gore in a fantasy world where the most vicious killers are the winners." Well, I wonder where they got that idea!?! *(tosses magazine aside, starts playing video game)* After all, every day in school we pledge allegiance to a country created by a violent revolution while condoning lifelong slavery for forty percent of its population. Every day we drive past fields and woods where millions of Native people lived until they were massacred and driven off the land. Every day we eat tens of millions of pounds of slaughtered animal flesh, and, hey, you vegan goody-goodies, don't go thinking you're so superior — ever heard a cucumber scream as it's ripped out of the soil? And the bumper sticker you see on cars of so-called successful people: "Whoever dies with the most toys wins?" Gee, what's the lesson there, boys and girls? We're talking cut-throat, eat-or-be-eaten, food-chain do-whatever-it-takes-to-survive moral philosophy here. And that's *every* day in *every* part of the world! Yeh, uh-huh, my parents tell me video games are a waste of time, a substitute for real life. Wrong-o! Video games *are* real life — except you can turn a video game *off*.

ANYTHING BUT THIS

(looking in mirror, adjusting hair and eyebrows, fingering nose)
I'm not sure when I first started hating the way I look. I never
thought about it as a little kid. I don't remember even looking
in a mirror. Nobody ever said anything to me that was negative,
like, "Hey, Pinnochio!" or "Whoa, horse-face, get a saddle!"
like they did with some kids. In fact, nobody says anything negative to me now. *(turns profile, presses on cheek)* But I don't
like it. It's just not — not what I want. I see people on TV, in
magazines, commercials. I know they're models, I know they're
computerized, I know they're composites, I know they're not
real. But every time I look in the mirror I think of those other
faces. Those other bodies. And I want to be them. Or, no,
maybe I don't want to be them. *(lifts head, puts finger under
chin)* I just want to be anything but *this*

KEEPING IN SHAPE

(on floor, doing strenuous sit-ups) Ninety-nine! One hundred! *(stops)* Whoa, what a rush! No, I'm not trying out for a team. Just keeping in shape. Why? Because I am a self-actualized person! I am the master of this body. I am in control. It's good to be in control. When you're a teenager, there's not much you can actually control about your life, but I can control my body. *(jumps up, jogs in place)* Now, I'm not some fanatic like the steroid-junkie bodybuilders. But the body needs to be reined in, needs to be controlled, needs to be *disciplined! (stops jogging, stretches)* Guess I've been dieting off and on since I was, like, seven. Always heard mom say things like, "I hate my hips! My thighs are grotesque!" And dad would always laugh at people on TV, "Look at that piggy! Whoa, he's a real porker! Ha-ha-ha!" *(stops, clenches fists)* Pretty soon, with the right diet and enough sit-ups, people won't ever laugh at *me* like that. Not even my mom and dad. *(starts doing vigorous toe touches)* One! Two! Three!

FUR FIGHTS BACK

I thought my dad would understand. I mean, he always talks about being a big radical when he was young. Protest marches, love-ins, hey-hey-LBJ-how-many-kids-you-kill-today. So, last night, me and my posse made a major political statement. We heaved rocks through the window of Old Man Bender's butcher shop, cause it's part of the system that harms animals. We spray-painted slogans on his wall — "Don't Eat Meat! Death to Animal Killers! Fur Fights Back!" Then we shoved a big bag of dog dump through his mail slot. *(laughs)* And now my dad refuses to bail me out. He says it was just pointless vandalism. No, dad, vandalism always has a point. *(smacks fist into palm)* And it goes right up where you've parked your brain.

DRIVER'S ED

(talking into cell phone) Dad? Oh-wow, I thought I'd get the answering machine, you're usually still at work, and I — did I want to leave a message? Uhhh-ummm, not exactly, I just thought I'd, you know, say, "Hi!" So, hi! *(chuckles)* Just out driving around, had a couple errands, oh-no, I'm not driving now, no, never drive and talk on the phone, oh-no, not a problem, Dad, I'm completely *not* driving. Where am I? Uhhh-ummm, just, you know, taking a break. From driving. Yeh, on the side of the road, it's a safety thing, take a break once in awhile, keep your reflexes sharp. And you sure do need those sharp reflexes, oh-yeh, pardon? That noise? Uhhh-ummm, it's a truck, yeh, looks like a truck, definitely a truck. Right, a tow truck, sure is, how'd you guess? What's it towing? Uhhh-ummm, looks like a car, uh-huh, definitely a car. What kind? Let me get a closer look, it's sort of a four-door — wow, that's amazing — it *is* my car! Incredible! Oh-yeh, looks like a little scratch on the fender. Maybe both fenders. And the passenger side, yeh, gee whiz, I'm sure glad I'm standing at the side of the road, that looks pretty serious, well, not *too* serious — pardon? Well, I did have one question. Uhhh-ummm, do you think this will count against me getting my license next month?

HEY, YOU!

Hey, You! Yes, You! I'm talking to You! You know, *You!* As in The You Generation, or Generation Y. You're already bigger than the baby boom, almost 80 million of You born since 1979. Hey, it's Your world, just listen to the media talking about You: "Have it *Your* way. Obey *Your* thirst. It's the science of *You*. It's all about *You*." And they're right! You are about to inherit a world that *You* will rule! *You* will shape! *You* will permanently imprint with *Your* generation's dreams, fears, loves, hates, hopes, tears!

And the question You need to answer is: When Your time comes, will You be ready? Only You can know. Because only You will ever be the one You have to answer to for how Your world came to be.

NEW SHOES

This new kid at school kept coming to class with skinned up knees and arms. It seemed like nobody could fall down that much, so we figured he was maybe on drugs. Or maybe getting beat up at home. Turns out he didn't have a home. He lived at a homeless shelter with his mom. And his shoes were so worn out that the rubber part in front had come up and made him trip all the time. Eddie's dad manages a discount store and got him a pair of new shoes. He was real happy, but when Eddie took his old shoes to throw in the trash, he got real upset and grabbed them back. "I better hang onto them," he said. "There might be another kid come into the shelter doesn't have any shoes at all."

I CAN DO THAT

Okay! Any time you're ready. A-one, a-two, a-three — *(sings to tune of "Them Old Cotton Fields Back Home")* When was a little bitty baby, my mama would knock me with a ladle, in them old tuna fields back home!

How's that? I think a half step higher would suit my range a bit better, but I can do it any key. Oh, it's a great jingle! I love it! Did you write it? I figured! It's sensational! And I think I'd bring a unique sort of passion to the interpretation, a sort of insight, a sort of edge, if you wanted something like that. You don't? Okay! No passion, no insight, no edge, I can do that. We're done? Okay. You'll let me know then? Okay. No-no, thank *you*. Ciao! *(smiles, waves, takes a few steps to right, grimaces)* Just keep reminding yourself — humiliation, disgrace, complete absence of dignity — this is *exactly* how all the great actors started out!

CALL ME CHRIS

Call me Chris. I crave classic cat cards and corduroy cushions. I care conscientiously for culture and cultivate a cosmopolitan coterie of cumberbunds and Q-tips, keeping correct counsel and cautionary credit in case the carnival comes and carries crates of candles across the contiguous creek. *(looks at watch)* Cripes! Can we continue this conversation at a more cordial confine? Capital! I'll call you — collect.

TIDYING UP

(wiping off a counter with a towel) I don't mind doing chores around the house. I feel good when I'm tidying up and fixing stuff. Beats doing homework! And since we moved to this new town, it's taking me awhile to jump into things socially, if you know what I mean. *(wiping harder, more deliberately)* It's funny, but I actually do more cleaning than my mom, though she's working full-time now to bring in what the alimony and child support don't cover. She tells me to relax, and I get a little mad when she laughs at me sometimes and says, "You know, baby, you can't always clean up everything. Sometimes things get messy and they just stay that way." *(stops wiping)* "I know," I tell her. "I guess I just don't like standing around watching the mess get worse."

THINGS I'VE LEARNED

Things I've learned about life since becoming a teenager:

I am an egomaniac with a massive inferiority complex. I'm basically a negative person, and that's why I'm so happy. Sometimes my mind is like a bad neighborhood, and I should not go in there alone. When you choose the lesser of two evils, always remember it is still an evil. If you must choose between two evils, pick the one you've never tried before. You cannot save your butt and your face at the same time. If at first you don't succeed, destroy all evidence that you tried. Experience is something you never get until just after you need it. You never really learn to swear until you get your driver's license. Monday is a terrible way to spend one-seventh of your life. A clear conscience is typically the sign of a bad memory. Hard work pays off in the future, but laziness pays off now. The sooner you fall behind, the more time you'll have to catch up. And, finally, change is inevitable — except from a vending machine.

FOREIGN EXCHANGE

(speaking in marked foreign accent) Hey-hey, whassup phat dog! You salty! I be chillin! Let's bounce, homie! (chuckles) Boy, do I love American language! So inventive, so varied, so jiggy! My language has fewer words, and you're not allowed to deviate from the grammar. The way American young people talk, the language never stops growing, never stops moving, like a river that keeps splashing out one new stream after another, always changing shape and direction. So much humor! What's not so funny is how American young people think about the rest of the world. I have made good friends here in Indiana, but it bothers me a little that they don't know much about what's going on outside the U.S. Or care. Sure we like American fashion and music, but we have traditions and philosophies of our own. We don't make money a god. We don't worship famous people or feel we are no good because we are not rich or famous. We don't think everyone should be just like us in everything we do. In our country a person isn't important from the money they have. They're important from how they use money to make a better life for their family, their village, their people. Hey-hey, home slice, better get snappin! It's a new century, and Greenwood, Indiana, is not the cultural cookie cutter for the rest of the world. Noooo diggity!

PLEASE TELL ME

Please. . . tell me. . . Please tell me it's okay to not wear the same clothes as everybody else, or like the same music or have the same hairstyle. Please tell me it's okay to think my own thoughts and not feel I'm stupid and worthless. Please tell me it's okay if I laugh too loud or cry too hard or care too much. Please tell me it's okay if I don't find true love right this minute. Please tell me it's okay if I don't know what I'm going to be when I grow up. Please tell me it's okay to not be popular with everybody in school and that I don't have to hurt somebody else to be popular. Please tell me to be patient. Please tell me to hurry up. Please tell me to slow down and look up at the stars and dream about flying across the universe. Please tell me war is going to end and racism will stop and the present will become the future and leave the past behind and the dictionary won't carry words like *kill* or *greed* or *hate,* they'll be unlisted and forgotten when evil thoughts have met their fate. Please tell me I'm not always crazy. Please tell me things make sense. Please tell me I'm going to look back someday and think it was fun to be a teenager. Please tell me I'm not the only person who thinks like this. Please. . . tell me. . .

L.E. McCullough, class of 1970

L.E. McCullough is a graduate of Brebeuf Jesuit High School in Indianapolis, where he was first-chair alto sax in the concert band, winner of a National Merit Scholarship, and co-editor of the underground newspaper. His goal as a grown-up is to write books people read that might possibly somehow change their lives for the better, or at least make them think they have.